THE HISTORY OF
GIBBETING

THE HISTORY OF
GIBBETING
Britain's Most Brutal Punishment

SAMANTHA PRIESTLEY

PEN & SWORD
HISTORY

AN IMPRINT OF PEN & SWORD BOOKS LTD.
YORKSHIRE – PHILADELPHIA

First published in Great Britain in 2020 by
PEN AND SWORD HISTORY
An imprint of
Pen & Sword Books Ltd
Yorkshire – Philadelphia

ISBN 978 1 52675 518 6

Typeset in Times New Roman 11.5/14 by
Aura Technology and Software Services, India.
Printed and bound in the UK by TJ International

Pen & Sword Books Limited incorporates the imprints of Atlas, Archaeology,
Aviation, Discovery, Family History, Fiction, History, Maritime, Military, Military
Classics, Politics, Select, Transport, True Crime, Air World, Frontline Publishing,
Leo Cooper, Remember When, Seaforth Publishing, The Praetorian Press,
Wharncliffe Local History, Wharncliffe Transport, Wharncliffe True Crime and
White Owl.

For a complete list of Pen & Sword titles please contact
PEN & SWORD BOOKS LIMITED
47 Church Street, Barnsley, South Yorkshire, S70 2AS, England
E-mail: enquiries@pen-and-sword.co.uk
Website: www.pen-and-sword.co.uk

Or

PEN AND SWORD BOOKS
1950 Lawrence Rd, Havertown, PA 19083, USA
E-mail: Uspen-and-sword@casematepublishers.com
Website: www.penandswordbooks.com

Contents

Acknowledgments

I couldn't have written this book without the help and support of these people. Thank you to:

Clara Morgan, Sheffield Museums. Katherine Holmes, Lincoln library. Luke Skerritt and Polly Wilkinson, the Boston Guildhall Museum. Ruth Gatenby, Louth Museum. Richard Carter, the Norris Museum. Megan Evans, the Haselmere Museum. Tim Pestell, Norwich Castle Museum. Jonathan Wheeler, the National Museum of Wales. William Hallett, for your support, help, and patience.

Introduction

The story of gibbeting in Britain has an ending, but no beginning. Though we know when this terrible punishment was outlawed, we don't know when or why it began. Gibbeting describes the ghoulish practice of hanging a criminal in a body-shaped cage, or irons, and leaving them suspended there for all to see. Many reasons were given for gibbeting people. It was said to keep the body hanging between earth and heaven so the deceased couldn't pass over. In a largely religious society, this was seen as preventing the criminal from being resurrected come judgment day, and therefore preventing his soul from being reunited with his body in the afterlife. In reality it was a spectacle, newly gibbeted criminals drew crowds of onlookers and stalls were often set up turning the whole thing into an event. But most of all, gibbeting was performed as a warning. Gibbets were often left with their inhabitants rotting away inside them for years, sometimes decades. Cross the line and this is what will happen to you.

The practice of displaying criminals, or their body parts, for all to see has been common place throughout history, so it's not hard to surmise how this evolved. Gibbeting was certainly used in the Roman Empire and could perhaps have been a continuation of crucifixion, which also saw criminals' bodies left to rot on the cross. It's impossible to know how the practice of gibbeting started, or where, but it's likely that gibbeting came about amid a variety of other forms of execution and post-mortem punishments and practices. In pre-medieval times and right up to the Jacobite rebellion, the heads of enemies were paraded on spikes as a form of terror and also pride. Viewing punishment as both a deterrent and as justice has long been the human way. Perhaps from displaying the heads of traitors on spikes, we moved on to displaying the whole of a criminal's body in an iron cage. We don't know; but we do know that gibbeting, like other post execution punishments, was reserved for the most serious crimes. You may have been executed for something as slight as stealing a sheep in the eighteenth century, but you were only gibbeted if you were found guilty of murder, robbing the mail, or piracy – with one or two notable exceptions.

Gibbeting was a horrific form of torture when performed on live criminals, and a gruesome spectacle when performed following execution. The body was placed in a tight cage of chains or irons that fitted the body perfectly and was then hung from a 20–30 ft high wooden post. Gibbet cages were made individually and no two were the same; none were removed before the body had decayed and all that was left was bones and dust.

Before legislation was put in place, how a criminal was executed and treated was at the discretion of the authorities in his or her community. This meant inconsistent and unregulated practices, and records of what happened are sometimes sketchy and unreliable. The further back we look the less we know. So, who we gibbeted, and why, back in the days before strict record-keeping and law, is like a long a forgotten dream. We have fragments, but we can never know the whole of it.

In William Andrews' book *Bygone Punishments*, published 1899, there is mention of three men being hung in chains near Chapel-en-le-Frith in 1341 for robbery and violence.

In 1379 Edward Hewison, a private in the Earl of Northumberland's Light Horse, was tried and convicted of raping Louisa Bently. Reports say this happened in a field on the way to York as Louisa was walking to her place of work. Hewison was executed at York Castle and afterwards his body was hung upon a gibbet in the field where the offence had taken place. There is no mention of Louisa's murder in any reports, only the rape, which makes it a highly unusual case of gibbeting. It also tells us that even in 1379 we executed criminals before we hung them in chains. Though, perhaps, not always.

This from Henry Chauncy's Historical Antiquities of Hertfordshire tells us that gibbeting has been taking place in Britain for many hundreds of years:

> Soon after the King came to Easthampstead, to recreate himself with hunting, where he heard that the bodies which were hanged here were taken down from the gallows, and removed a great way from the same; this so incensed the

King that he sent a writ, tested the 3rd of August, Anno 1381, to the bailiffs of this borough, commanding them upon sight thereof, to cause chains to be made, and to hang the bodies in them upon the same gallows, there to remain so long as one piece might stick to another, according to the judgement; but the townsmen, not daring to disobey the King's command, hanged the dead bodies of their neighbours again, to their great shame and reproach, when they could not get any other for any wages to come near the stinking carcasses, but they themselves were compelled to do so vile an office.

These are some of the earliest mentions of gibbeting in Britain, but they suggest it was already a known and used practice. It also gives us a good idea of how awful bodies hanging in chains was for the people who had to live and work near them.

Hanging in chains, whatever its origin, does seem to have been prevalent in Britain in medieval times and beyond. It was mostly used as a punishment for treason, with some murderers also being gibbeted, but by the eighteenth century at least this had shifted and we were hanging criminals in chains mostly for barbarous murder, and sometimes highway robbery and robbing the mail. Mostly, but not always. We may have used the post-mortem punishment of gibbeting through history, but there were no rules. These were the days when communities often took matters into their own hands and would punish people in ways we find abhorrent today, and also sometimes in ways that had been already outlawed. In 1752 in Sussex, Ann Whale was sentenced to death for murdering her husband. Her punishment was to be tied to a stake, first strangled to death and then her body burned till it was ashes. In 1753 in Gloucester, Ann Williams was burned at the stake for poisoning her husband. Her trial date was 10 April that year and by the seventeenth she was tied to a stake and burned alive, a practice that had already been abolished in 1656 for murder (burning alive for adultery still remained). Both of these cases took place after the Murder Act came into force in 1752, and used executions and punishments that were outlawed.

With so much unchecked lawlessness, and communities often calling for harsh punishments and tough justice, punishments for crimes were wildly inconsistent. Even after the Murder Act came into force, laws were flouted in small communities and when it came to punishing those who had done wrong, we could be vicious and unmerciful.

All of this does need perspective. Britain was a very different place and punishments like gibbeting were very rare. The fact that they existed at all may shock us today, but at the time it was seen as necessary and just.

Our journey through the history of gibbeting in Britain is a sad and astounding one and may cause us to look uncomfortably, with a side-long glance, at our ancestors and what they did.

Chapter 1

The Murder Act

Bleak moorland, craggy hills, a shoreline battered by wild seas. Christian churches and pagan festivals. Fields that sweep ahead as far as sight allows. Rumbling clouds above, white, grey and then black. Valleys and still lakes and roads that snake through land like a dog nosing forward, blind to what lies ahead. Mist rises in the morning and the air is stark. A bell tolls. Scones and jam, the village green, the woods thick and dark People live in pockets of small communities and practice old customs and tightly rooted traditions. There is a constant shifting feeling of appearances slipping and exposing what lies beneath. The land and the people live together with suspicion and whispers of what went before. This is Britain. Often romanticised, but also recognised as the strange and eerie place it is. We live on a small island, disconnected from vast mainland, strange tales intensify and all that goes bump in the night somehow seems louder, though we try to stifle it.

Our green and pleasant land has long been depicted in songs, films, books, and poems, and its darker side is often exposed and even celebrated. M.R. James's short story, *a View From a Hill*, perfectly captures this placing of all that is beautiful in Britain besides all that is dark and terrible. In the story two friends go for an evening walk in the surrounding countryside, in what is a local beauty spot. They describe the wheat fields and pretty hedges, the delicate scattered cottages, the smell of hay and roses and the disappearing steam from a train whisping in the breeze. But when one of the men raises his binoculars to the hill beyond, he sees something unsettling and disturbing. A body hanging in its gibbet, placed on the crest of the hill for everyone below to see. The body sways menacingly in its creaking chains and while farmers tend to their livestock and their land and the people go about their business, this ghastly reminder of the darkness all around us prevails and lives side by side with the beauty and goodness.

1

It seems unthinkable to us now, but this was the reality in many areas of Britain. And what's worse, while we went about our everyday lives and lived in the beauty of our land, we also revelled in the spectacle of live hangings and gibbetings. We were a vengeful, bloodthirsty people. Charles Dickens, on witnessing a public hanging, talked of the appalling way the people flocked to the spectacle and behaved as if it was a carnival. He stated that the execution and the crime that led to it was nothing in comparison to the way people conducted themselves around it. Rather than live hangings and gibbetings giving people a sense of justice being done and an end being put to the matter, we seem to have behaved worse around these spectacles, as if the evil in the situation bled into us as witnesses, and we celebrated the gruesome punishment and found ourselves dragged down by it.

The Murder Act, or 'An act for better preventing the horrid crime of murder' came into force in 1752, and it included direct instructions on the gibbeting of murderers. There had been a long period of debate in the run up to the Murder Act over which punishments fitted which crimes and how we could, as a society, better prevent those crimes from being committed in the first place. It must have been difficult to negotiate the shape of all this, as punishments for crimes committed had so far been confusing and very changeable. Many officials believed that the punishment should fit the crime, so, loosely speaking, the criminal would be subjected to a punishment of the same proportion as the crime. If a person was guilty of assault on another person by beating, as punishment they would be beaten also. On the face of it this is direct justice, but it was difficult to enforce and keep track of, and it opened up all kinds of problems of misuse. And what of murderers? Some murders are more shocking, more evil, than others. While murder was punishable by death, it was felt that some murderous crimes were too terrible for even this to be enough, and the idea of mutilating bodies after death seemed appropriate. There were few prisons and it was cheaper and easier to either execute criminals, or give them a beating then let them go, than it was to incarcerate them. No thought seems to have been given to the inevitability that mistakes would be made. Or if it had, the cost of gaoling prisoners and the attitude of 'tough justice' prevailed. For those who had been wrongly convicted and executed, and for their families, there was no justice, and there seemed no end to the dark times of blood for blood

The Murder Act states that it is at the discretion of the judge in each case to decide, but that provision was made for hanging the murderer's body in chains following their execution. In other words, it not only solidifies in law what we had already been doing for hundreds of years, it specifies bodies can be, and perhaps should be, gibbeted. Or at least that's how it was sometimes interpreted. Its vagueness caused confusion, especially after the Anatomy Act was passed in 1832 which opened up the possibility of dissection on bodies other than those of murderers; until this time only the bodies of murderers could be sent for dissection. Their bodies were to be either dissected or gibbetted, but certainly not buried. The Anatomy Act recognised the need for more bodies to be dissected and stated that the unclaimed bodies of the poor could also be taken for dissection.

The Murder Act – still in force at this time – stated that the bodies of murderers had to be either dissected or hung in chains, so when the vague wording of the Anatomy Act stated that the bodies of the poor were now to be dissected, some judges mistook this as meaning murderers *had* to be hung in chains because there was no other option:

> Provided also, That it shall be in the power of any such judge or justice to appoint the body of any such criminal to be hung in chains: but that in no case whatsoever the body of any murderer shall be suffered to be buried; unless after such body shall have been dissected and anatomized as aforesaid; and every such judge or justice shall, and is hereby required to direct the same either to be disposed of as aforesaid, to be anatomized, or to be hung in chains, in the same manner as is now practiced for the most atrocious offences.

Before the Anatomy Act, if the body of an executed murderer wasn't to be gibbeted it was to be sent to surgeons for dissection, which was much more likely and usual. The Murder Act contains a large paragraph on bodies of murderers being sent for dissection and this is placed near the beginning, so it seems this was the preferred method of dealing with murderers.

There is much talk in the Act of how terrible a crime murder is and the language used is very persuasive and full of impact. The thrust of it is that the post-mortem punishments are there as a very visible show. Post-mortem punishments were to inflict further horror in the mind of the criminal and also the community, and would also show very publicly that justice is done:

> the marks of infamy hereby directed for such offenders, in order to impress a just horror in the mind of the offender, and on the, minds of such as shall be present, of the heinous crime of murder.

But there are no directions to suggest which murderers should be given which punishments. It seems to say that hanging in chains should only be used as an option if dissection isn't possible, rather than as a more severe punishment. The option is there, but it is presented as a lesser option to dissection and isn't given the status of horror and justice we might expect. It also seems to suggest the reason for continuing to hang in chains is one of tradition – this is done already and so we'll continue with the practice.

While gibbeting the corpses of executed criminals is gruesome enough, before the Murder Act came into force in the eighteenth century there was nothing stopping anyone from gibbeting people alive. There are folk tales and stories of live gibbetings having taken place in Britain, and although it's believable that this happened, we don't have any actual evidence of it. Considering our history of gruesome torture and horrific ways of executing criminals, it's likely this did occur. It was 'acceptable' to inflict many different forms of punishment on convicted criminals, and we certainly did. Stories of live gibbeting are sketchy, but still compelling.

Live gibbeting has certainly been used as a form of slow execution in other parts of the world. In 838 in Iran, Babak Khorramdin was gibbeted alive and his hands and feet were cut off. As late as January 1921 *The National Geographic* magazine printed two photos that showed gibbet cages in use in Afghanistan. The report that accompanied the photos stated that these were used for gibbeting criminals alive. It could easily have been the evolution of crucifixion, as hanging a criminal up and letting them slowly and painfully starve to death is essentially what crucifixion was, so why not put them in chains and do this? At least it ensures the body stays up there.

While some reports suggest that this may have happened, it's hard to tie the facts down. In 1551 in Kent, Mrs Arden was having a passionate affair with a man named Mosbie, so passionate in fact, she decided she needed to get rid of her husband so she could be with her lover. Mrs Arden had money and finding someone who would murder her husband for a fee wasn't difficult. This involved a few co-conspirators, most of whom would end up executed for the crime. When her husband was killed, Mrs Arden and her conspirators were quickly rounded up and sentenced to death. If we look at the gang's crimes and their punishments we can see how foggy the appointing of punishments could be. There's no doubt that the murder was Mrs Arden's idea and she was sentenced to death by burning alive, but punishments for the other conspirators seem wildly inconsistent. Mrs Arden's maid was also burned alive, presumably for being privy to the plan. Mosbie and his sisters, also in on the plan, were all hanged. It was Mosbie and his accomplice, a 'ruffian' named Black Will, who were in the room when Mr Arden was murdered, and while Black Will held Mr Arden down with a towel around his head, it was Mosbie who struck him with a heavy iron until he died. Mosbie complained on his arrest that he never wanted to do this, but still admitted that he had. Black Will was apprehended some time later in Holland and burned alive. This left Michael, Mr Arden's manservant, and Green, an acquaintance of Mosbie, who were both in on the plan and helped to bring it all together. These two men were certainly guilty of conspiring to murder, but they were not the instigators and they were not present when the deed was done. And yet it was these two alone who were hung in chains. It's not clear whether these two men were executed first or not. Michael was hanged in chains at Faversham and Green was hanged in chains in the highway between Ospringe and Boughton, near Faversham. This extract found in the book *Old Ballads* by Thomas Evans, published in 1810, is taken from a popular ballad of the time and suggests they were gibbeted alive, but a suggestion is all we have: 'At Fethersham were hanged in chains and well rewarded for their faithful pains … In Kent at Osbringe Green did suffer death, hanged on a gibbet he did lose his breath.'

Only the absence of the details about exactly how they were executed leads us to imagine live gibbeting could have happened here. In reports from the period, there is no mention of these two men being hanged first, only of them being hung in chains, while Mosbie was certainly hanged and not gibbeted at all. This leads to many questions, for which we can only guess at answers. Why were these two men chosen to be gibbeted and hung up as an example and a deterrent, while the others were not? How did we decide who would be hung in chains and why did we do this?

Whether we always executed criminals before we hung them in chains, or if sometimes one was hung up and left to die in his body shaped cage, we simply don't know. In the case of John Keale, who murdered his wife and child in Louth, Lincolnshire, in 1731, there is evidence that we did not, at this time, gibbet alive. A contemporary pamphlet detailing the case, states:

> Both before at and after his trial and condemnation at the Lent assize in the county hall of Lincoln on Tuesday the 7th march 1731 by the Lord Baron Page, by whom he was deservedly condemned to be gibbeted alive for a most horrid and bloody murder committed on the body of his wife and young child in September last … though the judge pronounced sentence that he should be gibbeted alive, yet the laws of England allow for no such death, therefore he was taken from Lincoln in a light cart and the gibbet irons with him and with very little ceremony hanged upon a gibbet post by the neck till he was dead, when cut down he was put into the irons and again hung up, between earth and heaven, food for every devouring bird of prey.

It's interesting that it states that the laws allow for no such death, but there were also no such laws preventing it. There were no laws about gibbeting at all before the Murder Act. However, the mere fact that the judge in this case desired to gibbet John Keale alive suggests that this is something he knew of and perhaps something he knew had happened. John Keale had committed a most terrible murder. A heavy drinker, he came home one evening and started a row with his wife, accusing her of having an affair and of bearing him a son that wasn't his; his anger got the better of him. He chopped off the baby's head and then stabbed his wife to death. It's easy to see why the judge in this case sought the most extreme punishment possible, but not so easy to decipher why he ultimately decided against it.

Let's say we did gibbet alive. This meant hanging the person in the body-shaped iron cage and leaving them there to die of starvation while birds pecked away at their flesh. The person in the gibbet would have been rendered completely immobile by the cage and would have hung in the cold waiting for death to take them. It's doubtful many of them would have waited quietly. Everyone who entered a gibbet alive would only emerge again once they were a skeleton – and then sometimes not completely. There have been numerous gibbets still containing the skulls of their victims unearthed in Britain and around the world, and as gibbet irons fitted the body of the criminal exactly, once the flesh had rotted away and fallen, the bones of the skeleton would have slipped through the irons if they detached. The skull of Sion y Gof was excavated still in its head irons in Wales in 1938, and John Bread's skull remains in its gibbet today, tucked away in the attic of Rye Museum. Once the gibbet was eventually taken down, sometimes decades later, what was left of the unhappy skeleton was buried unmarked, usually right there at the site of the gibbet. What happened to the rest of them may be even more gruesome, as family members and souvenir-seekers often made off with what fell from the gibbet.

Two Tales of Live Gibbeting

At Caxton Gibbet, a small hill between London and Huntington, it's said a man was gibbeted alive for murdering another man called Partridge some time in the 1670s. We have very little to go on in this sparse story and details vary depending on who tells it. We don't even have the name of the murderer, only the name of the man who was murdered, which is very unusual. Some accounts say Partridge was murdered for killing the other man's dog, while others say he was a poacher and murdered for poaching on someone else's land. Either way, the story goes, the murderer of Partridge suffered the unhappy fate of being locked in an iron cage and left to die there.

While it's impossible to say how long we were doing this for, if we did it at all, we do still hold the story of the last person said to be gibbeted alive. Unfortunately his name has been lost to history too, just like Partridge's killer, but he was gibbeted in the seventeenth century on what is now gruesomely named 'Gibbet Moor' in the Peak District.

Baslow is a quaint and quiet village in Derbyshire's Peak District and at the time of this occurrence in the seventeenth century there were less than 1,000 people living there. When a homeless man, desperately hungry and searching for shelter, came wandering through this pretty little village, nobody could have predicted the changes his actions would set in motion. The man was going from house to house asking for donations of food and when he reached a row of thatched cottages in the village the smell of frying bacon led him straight to one cottage in particular.

The beggar knocked on the door as the delicious scent of the meat wafted in the air and made his stomach gurgle. The lady who lived in this house answered the door and told him she had just finished cooking and eating her breakfast and the bacon he could smell was all gone. Whether she had any other food to give this desperate man or not, she told him she had nothing for him and attempted to turn him away. But the smell of the bacon must have been too much for the starving vagrant who forced his way into the house. No matter how weak he might have been from the cold and hunger, he overpowered the woman who lived in the cottage and poured the boiling fat from the bacon straight down her throat. The poor woman was scalded and burned to death. A grisly way to go.

The man must have caused such a commotion he was immediately arrested and sentenced to an equally grisly death. He was gibbeted alive on Gibbet Moor, close to where his crime had been committed. The beggar was hung in the body-hugging iron cage and left there on the desolate moor to die. But this man didn't go quietly, he wasn't giving up just yet. It's said that a passing traveller gave him some food and mistakenly prolonged his torture, and as the wind rocked the gibbet and the cold entered his bones, and the birds pecked at his loose flesh, the man screamed and shouted for mercy. There was no mercy to be had from the gibbet or those who enforced this terrible punishment, but some good did come of this man's loud and noisy wait for death.

As the Duke of Devonshire tried to sleep in nearby Chatsworth House the screams of the dying man battered his windows and kept him from slumber. According to legend he was so tired of hearing the noise from the gibbet, the duke personally intervened and helped to put an end to live gibbeting in Britain. The story doesn't quite end there. Although we don't know the names of the homeless man or the woman he murdered, they aren't lost forever. A hiker was making her way over Gibbet Moor in 1992 when she reportedly heard the eerie screams of the unfortunate vagrant, his ghost still suspended in his gibbet hanging between earth and heaven. And it's not only the gibbeted man whose soul isn't at rest. The murdered woman is said to sit at the side of the bed in the master bedroom of her cottage. The librarian and archivist at Chatsworth House, Edar Osbourne, who died in 1978, told of a ghostly woman who soothed him when he was bedridden with illness. He believed this to be the murdered woman who had refused the homeless man some food when he came begging. While the two ghosts of Baslow, the gibbeted man forever reliving the torment of the gibbet and his victim making amends by giving endless kindness, haunt the landscape of this pretty Derbyshire village, a more tangible consequence of what happened here has gone down in history.

This, then, was the last man said to be gibbeted alive in Britain, or so the story goes. Following the torturous punishment and his horrendous screaming, we decided this was too barbarous a punishment, or we as spectators and the ones who had to live with this horrendous slow death, decided we didn't want to witness it anymore. Whether these stories have any basis in truth, we can't know, and tales of live gibbetings are so sparse and have so little link to actual documentation, they are only half-remembered dreams. But we do know for certain that in documented cases we executed criminals first before we hung them up in chains. However, this was still at the discretion of a judge in each community. The Bloody Code, the English legal system that ran from the late seventeenth century to the early nineteenth century, included 215 crimes punishable by death by the time it ended in 1820. A series of legal acts meant more and more crimes were added to the list of those punishable by death as time went on. But for the majority of cases judges chose not to pass the sentence of death. When they did, there was no law in place for how they disposed of the bodies or how they further punished them after death. Until 1752 when the Murder Act was passed.

Records from before the Murder Act was introduced do indeed show the need for such an Act. Punishments for crimes varied wildly and often seem incredibly disproportionate and scattered. If we take the county of Gloucestershire from 1727 until the time of The Murder Act, we can see how rare gibbeting was, but also the huge disparity between punishments for crimes. While murder was punishable by death, manslaughter was punishable by 'burning in the hand'. This was part of an old Anglo-Saxon law that meant being branded on the thumb with a letter relating to your offence. M for manslaughter, for example. To be burned in the hand can't have been pleasant, but those who were returned a verdict of manslaughter rather than murder must have thanked their lucky stars indeed. It was a very fine line they walked. Branding as a punishment wasn't formally abolished until 1822. The accounts from the Gloucester Journals also show that before the Murder Act was passed, we were certainly executing criminals before we gibbeted them. There is not one single case of live gibbeting in the county of Gloucestershire. The main difference seems to lie in the location of execution. It's often stated in these accounts that criminals were executed at the place of the crime and then hung in chains there too, rather than the later practice of criminals being hanged at the county gaol and then transported back to the scene of the crime to be hung in their gibbet irons. In some early cases, reports talk of criminals facing the tree they would be hung from, rather than a constructed gallows, and the terror that struck them at the sight of nature's own gibbet post. The murderous gang members William Blewitt and Emanuel Dickinson wept bitterly at the place of execution, the fatal tree. These were career criminals, part of a gang of daring robbers who operated across London and would murder anyone who stood in their way. When they were taken to their execution in 1726 William and Emmanuel showed much remorse at the sight of the tree. Following their hanging they were taken back to the gaol at Southwark where they were fitted for their irons, and then transported on a cart back to St George's Fields where they were hung in their gibbets. Not all prisoners approached their death in this way. William Alcock, who murdered his wife in 1733, was a jovial character till the very end it seems, as *The Newgate Calendar* recorded at the time of his execution:

> On the road to the gallows he sung part of the old song of Robin Hood, adding to each verse, the chorus of derry down, &c. At intervals he swore, kicked, and spurned, at any person who touched the cart. When tied up to the fatal tree, he kicked off his shoes, to avoid a well known proverb; and being told by a person in the cart with him, and who wished, thus late, to reclaim him, that he had much better read and

repent, than thus vilely swear and sing, he struck the book out of this humane man's hands, damned the spectators, and called for wine.

To be hanged from a tree, prisoners would have climbed a ladder to reach the branch from which they would hang. Sometimes two trees were used, a beam fixed between them and a ladder leaned against the beam. Sometimes the hangman would manually haul the prisoner up onto the noose hanging from the tree. When this was followed by hanging in chains with no other site involved it was a seamless process, all conducted at the same tree. Presumably this would have meant the bodies being placed in their gibbet irons immediately after execution, as one continuous spectacle, with eager crowds watching the entire procedure. But this is by no means constant. Depending on the county and town or village of execution, and the year, some were hanged from a tree at the location of the crime and then hung from their gibbet post in chains; sometimes a gibbet post was erected for the hanging and then the gibbeting on the same post, while some were hung at an appointed place of law and then taken to the scene of the crime for the gibbet. As time went on the latter took over and the former stopped making an appearance.

Trees were used as gallows in Anglo-Saxon times and the Triple Tree at Tyburn was still in use as a gallows in 1759. In 1783 executions began taking place at Newgate Prison. In other parts of Britain it was some time later that this happened. The Heavitree gallows in Devon, at the junction between the Honiton and Sidmouth Roads, was still used as a place of public executions until 1798 when executions were moved to Exeter prison. In York, Knavesmire had been the site of public hangings since 1379. Often known as the York Tyburn, named after the famous Middlesex gallows, Dick Turpin was hanged here. The last public hanging took place at this location in 1801 on a constructed gallows, following the earlier method of the tree. It was thought that this public place for hanging was creating a bad impression to visitors of the city and at this point hangings were moved to York Castle. In Winchester, public hangings had traditionally taken place at Gallows Hill near the Jolly Farmer Inn. The last recorded public hanging at Gallows Hill was in 1819 and was of Sarah Huntington who had murdered her husband. The Jolly Farmer Inn still stands today. In 1830 John Dyke was publicly hanged at Penenden Heath in Kent, a site for public hangings since Anglo-Saxon times. Following this last hanging on the heath, executions in this area were moved to Maidstone Prison. After 1830, public hangings were taking place at castles and gaols all over the country and the fateful tree, as well as constructed gallows in public locations, had ceased to be used for executions.

Parson Darby and the Yew Tree

At Darby Green near Yately in Hampshire there stands a glorious old yew tree in the front garden of a row of old higgledy-piggledy cottages. These are Yew Tree Cottages and this is the famous tree from which a local figure named Parson Darby was hanged as a highwayman. There are a few historical contenders for who Parson Darby might have been – the Reverend Richard Lewen, the Revered John Tooley-Hawley, the Reverend John Thomas, Claud Duval, and William Davis (the golden farmer). As Claud Duval was hanged at Tyburn for his highway activity, it's unlikely to have been him. Richard Lewen and John Thomas seemingly died natural deaths so it's unlikely to have been either of them. John Tooley-Hawley is more of a mystery. He was a womaniser and had to leave his post as reverend after his 'revolting' indiscretions with parishioners came to light. What happened to him after this isn't known, and a womaniser doesn't make a highwayman.

The most likely candidate seems to be William Davis, who had many aliases and was a career criminal. However, although William was gibbeted in the area he was certainly hanged in London and not at Darby Green. In all research done on this captivating story there are no records anywhere of a parson in the area with the name Darby, so who he really was we'll never know. What we do know is that there was a man going by that name who was a reverend by day and a highwayman by night. This busy entrepreneur also had a love of the ladies and it's said that one woman, whom he had wooed and then abandoned, finally gave up his double life to the authorities. Parson Darby may have been an alias, or the story of what happened here could have passed into folklore and been altered so much we no longer hold the truth, but the yew tree is still there today. Parson Darby, whoever he was, was caught, possibly drinking in what was then the Yew Tree Arms, and taken out and hanged from the strong branches of the tree. So much of what happened here is lost to hearsay but there is a Gibbet Lane in nearby Camberley, so it's possible Parson Darby was gibbeted there. We don't have any records of who else might have been gibbeted there. What we do know is that this village is now named Darby Green and local historians connect this directly with the story of Parson Darby.

In the years following the introduction of the Murder Act gibbeting seems to have become more popular and, perhaps because of its random use and because there was so much debate about how to treat serious criminals, the need for the Murder Act would have been apparent. But it's sometimes hard to see, both before the Murder Act and after, how and why some criminals were chosen to be gibbeted and some were not.

The Case of William Elby

William Elby, sometimes Dunn, was a career criminal who spent many years thieving from anyone he could in some very inventive and unusual ways. But as William progressed in his dark career and came into contact with other hardened criminals, he clearly became more cruel and more merciless. William had worked with a number of other burglars and thieves, most of whom had already been caught at some point and had been hanged for their crimes. This didn't put Elby off and he continued with his lifestyle. In 1704 one of Elby's accomplices, William Stanley, murdered John Elliot in a robbery gone wrong. Poor John was simply in the wrong place at the wrong time and as the pair of thieves ran from a shop to the cries of 'stop thief', John Elliot attempted to apprehend them, for which he received a knife through the stomach and died. Elby witnessed all this and would have been aware that William Stanley was hanged for the crime, but still this didn't put Elby off and he became even more unruly and unpredictable. When at last he broke into a house and, during a struggle, killed the servant Nicholas Hatfield, Elby was caught and sentenced to death. Perhaps because he had persisted for so long and perhaps because he had already been imprisoned at Newgate a couple of times with no charges brought, Elby would receive the worst punishment available. William Elby was finally executed and hung in chains at Fulham on 13 September 1707. He was 32 when he died and had been a criminal since his young apprenticeship as a clockmaker.

But why did the authorities decide to gibbet Elby and not Stanley? The murders were very similar. Both had been robberies gone wrong. Neither had been premeditated murder. Both took place when the murderer was faced with being caught by someone standing in his way of carrying out the robbery. Both were by stabbing. The only reason seems to be one of perceived justice. Elby had been getting away with his criminal lifestyle for years, so he deserved a punishment that went that little bit further than simple hanging. He was perhaps made an example of, but it feels more like this was done to show that the authorities understood the need for the extra punishment. Perhaps he was a known career criminal in the community. Perhaps it was done to appease the people.

This does seem to have come into play quite often, and in the case of a constable by the name of Rosevear in 1720, gibbeting seems to have been carried out as a warning, a show of strength, and as a signal to the people in the community that Rosevear was indeed getting what was coming to him. From *The History of Cornwall* Hitchins and Drew:

> We are told that he was hanged at Launceston for his part in a Tinners Riot at Par demanding grain from a store house waiting to be shipped. At the time he was a constable. He was publicly hanged and his body taken to St Austell Downs where he was suspended on the Gibbet to 'blacken in the sun and furnish meat for birds of prey'.

Rosevear was a constable, driven by hunger to take part in a riot in the hope of procuring some grain. He was certainly made an example of and the last line stating he was to be meat for birds is particularly blood-thirsty. As a constable he was trusted by the people of his community and there would have been a need to show them that his behaviour wouldn't be tolerated. What better way than to hang his body in irons for the birds to peck at, humiliating him and serving as a reminder to the people that justice had been done.

This is one of very few cases of gibbeting that didn't come as a result of murder, robbing the mail, or highway robbery, and it can only be guessed that it was the fact that Rosevear was a constable that sealed his fate this way. There are other cases of gibbeting that were not strictly as a result of murder, highway robbery, or robbing the mail, and the use of the punishment in these cases does drive home the randomness of the practice. In 1597 John Thomas De Neim was executed and hung in chains on Hewith Moor, Yorkshire, for robbing Eugene Peit with 'intent to murder'. Similarly the following year Thomas Henry de Alting and Thomas Swedier were executed and hung in chains in Knaresborough Forest for housebreaking with 'intent to murder'. These two crimes and their punishments could be a consequence of the times in which they were committed, the punishment is still confusing when, just two years later in the same area, a gang of smugglers who did commit murder were executed and sent for dissection. And 200 years later in 1794, Patrick Quin and Patrick Coine were both executed for burgling the house of Benjamin Catcutt in Northwoord, The Isle of Wight, with 'the intent to murder'. Both men were hanged at Southampton and then taken by boat back to Northwood where their bodies were hung in chains, showing that these exceptions to the rule continued for a long time. Just why these men were hung in chains for burglary with threat, while some murderers were merely hanged, is baffling.

Although the majority of cases of hanging in chains were as a result of murder, the waters are still muddy at times. Who was hung in chains was a decision for the authorities in that parish, but with crowds of people attending public hangings, punishments also had to be seen as just by the community. If the authorities got this wrong, angry crowds would soon let them know. In some cases it also appears to have been about who the victim was – and equally, who the murderer was.

The Case of The Goodiers

From the Gloucester Journals:

> 1741
> Jan 27. Bristol, Jan 20. Account of the murder of SIR JOHN DINELEY GOODIER, of Charleton, Evesham, aboard the RUBY Man of War, by the Captain, his brother, and CHARLES WHITE (of IRL) and MATTHEW MAHONY (of IRL); Coroner's Inquest, Wilful Murder. Mar 31. Gloucester, Mar 28. We hear from Bristol, that this Day Capt. GOODIER, MATTHEW MAHONY, and CHARLES WHITE, received Sentence of Death for the barbarous

Murder of Sir JOHN GOODIER, Bart. The Captain's Trial lasted upwards of 8 hours.

Apr 7. London, Apr 4. Capt. GOODIER, WHITE and MAHONY, are order'd to be hanhg'd the 15th Inst. At Bristol, for the Murder of Sir JOHN DINELEY GOODIER, Bart.

Apr 14. Bristol, Apr 4. Capt. GOODERE, MATTHEW MAHONY, and CHARLES WHITE, for the Murder of Sir JOHN DINELEY GOODERE
      This Week a Smith took Measure of MATTHEW MAHONEY, for his Chains, he alone being order'd to be hang'd in Chains some where down the River.

Apr 21. Last Wednesday Capt. GOODERE, MATTHEW MAHONY, and CHARLES WHITE, for the Murder of Sir JOHN DINELEY GOODERE, Bart. were executed at St Michael's Hill, Bristol. The Captain went thither in a Mourning Coach, the other three in a Cart; and all confess'd the Crimes for which they suffer'd. MAHONY dy'd a Roman Catholick. The next Day the Captain's Body was put into a Hearse, and carry'd into Herefordshire, to be interr'd there; and the Body of MAHONY has since been hung in Chains.

Why was Mahoney alone hung in chains for this premeditated and cruel murder? This case does have some logic to it, although we may still have some sympathy for Mahoney. Samuel Goodier had resolved to murder his brother for the common reason of money. Sir John Goodier had it all, a title, an inheritance and a beautiful wife, while Samuel had none of these things. John was the eldest brother so it may seem fair that he was the one to benefit the most from their father's death, but Samuel certainly didn't think so.

Accounts suggest that John Goodier was not a good husband and when his wife sought affection elsewhere he sought to ruin her, though would not grant her the divorce she wanted. Samuel may have been aware of his brother's ungentlemanly behaviour and he may have seen this as further reason to do away with him, or it could have been simply a stab at getting his hands on the fortune. Samuel planned the murder, but he wasn't about to get his own hands dirty. He enlisted some sailors to help him carry out the deed and once onboard the *Ruby Man Of War*, Charles White and Michael Mahoney set about John Goodier. White held him down and Mahoney strangled him with a length of cord. So, it was Mahoney who murdered John Goodier. Technically. Though it could be said they all had a hand in it. It does seem at first glance that this is fair and just, Mahoney was the one who carried out the deed of murder while the other two men held the victim down and guarded the door. However, it does also present the question of why we were gibbeting. The three men were hanged and then Mahoney alone suffered the indignity of being hung in chains.

Was this a form of justice? It doesn't seem to make sense that it was done as a deterrent as there were three men involved in the plot and the murder, and if anyone was guilty of the premeditation of murder if was Samuel. Hanging the murderer in chains seems to have been a much more vengeful act in this case. Perhaps because of who Sir John Goodier was and his standing in the community. It's worth considering what the mood surrounding this murder would have been and how it would have been perceived, and also how high the demand for blood in return for blood would have been.

While gibbeting has been used in a few rare cases for other crimes, and was also used for criminals who robbed the mail or carried out highway robbery, it was usually reserved for criminals who had murdered and even then, it was normally a very gruesome or barbaric murder that called for such a punishment. The 'eye for an eye' mentality of the time often dictated punishments and while we had ceased taking this too far by this time in our history – we no longer went to the lengths of drowning a murderer who had killed by drowning – we did still feel the need to punish proportionately. Hanging for murder was a fair punishment, but hanging for brutal and vicious murder was not enough. The case of Henry Brookman is such a case if ever there was one.

1727

It was January when Mary Cuff died. The air would have been cold enough to see the puff of breath in front of her face and as she walked to the Quaker meeting house as often she did; she would have had no idea that someone in her village could be so vicious, and to her. Mary was a devout woman and completely undeserving of such a heinous act. Henry Brookman, on the other hand, was said to be idle and would rather thieve and take all he could than work, or spend any time in quiet contemplation on his life and the things he did. It was a Wednesday when Henry Brookman killed Mary Cuff and left her body on the ground inside the Quaker meeting house. Such an act was shocking enough, and the sight of poor Mary's body in this building that was reserved for peace would have caused a panic to ripple through every member of the community, but it was the viciousness of this attack that really stuck in the throats of everyone who knew Mary. Once the news was out that Mary had been murdered in the meeting house a neighbour quickly came forward and told of seeing Henry walking from the building at that time. Henry was swiftly apprehended and searched and the money, plus a bloody knife, was found on his person.

Henry Brookman was only 18 years of age when he brutally murdered Mary Cuff. He stabbed her with a knife he had taken there specifically for the purpose, then slit her throat from ear to ear. Although Henry would plead that his hunger had driven him to do this, and he had indeed robbed Mary of all the money she had on her, which was a paltry amount, the fact that Henry had taken a knife to the woman and mercilessly killed her before attempting to rob her ultimately sealed his fate.

There was no way to wriggle out of this situation and Henry duly confessed to knocking Mary to the ground, stabbing her and slitting her throat in a totally unprovoked and barbarous attack, and then searching her pockets for what money he could steal. Henry would try to haggle inside his guilt and suggested that he had only gone there to rob the woman and that he had found the knife in her possession, but nobody believed that he had not taken the terrifying weapon with him with the exact intention of killing for money. The judge at Henry's trial produced the only punishment he knew that could possibly fit such a horrendous murder; 18-year-old Henry Brookman was executed on Hursley Hill near the meeting house where Mary was murdered and then hung in chains on the same spot. From the Gloucester Inquests in *Gloucester Journal* 1722 to 1838:

> Bristol, Apr 8. We hear that at the Assizes at Taunton 10 Malefactors receiv'd Sentence of Death; among whom is HENRY BROOKMAN for the Murder of a poor Woman

at Belton Meeting House near Pensford, ... Brookman is to be executed on Wednesday next on a Gibbet near the said Meeting House, and to be hang'd up in Chains on the same.

Bristol, Apr 28. On Friday last about one in the Afternoon, HENRY BROOKMAN was executed, and afterwards hanged in Chains, on Hursley-hill, for the Murder of MARY CUFF, a Quaker. He confess'd the said Murder, and said he stabb'd her in seven Places, and then cut her Throat and robb'd her of 1s. 6d. Some Gentlemen having the Curiosity to ask him, why he was Guilty of such a Crime? He answered (as he did before the Judge) that 'twas Hunger made him do it.

This is a straightforward and easy to understand case. Sometimes, however, it's hard to figure why some murderers warranted gibbeting and some did not. Not all cases of murder that brought the sentence of hanging in chains appear to have been especially brutal, or at least not more brutal than other murders that carried a sentence of hanging alone.

The case of Roger Bryant tells of perhaps an unwilling murderer, perhaps an accidental murder. While there's no doubt that Bryant was a criminal, whether he was a brutal, merciless murderer isn't so clear. He certainly seems to have been repentant and was clearly distressed at the sight of the house where the event took place. Roger Bryant was only 24 when he became a murderer. He'd already deserted his position as a sheep shearer and then a foot soldier, not liking either employment and finding it difficult to get along with others and take orders from his masters. Roger had done some work for Tobias Luton who owned Toghill house farm, early in the year of 1727, but hadn't yet been paid for his labour. He arrived at the farmhouse one Sunday to ask for his payment, but Mr and Mrs Luton were at church and only the maid, Anne Williams, was at home. One way or another, Roger was determined to get his pay right there and then. Whether Anne let him enter the house or he forced his way inside, she must have protested at some point because Roger knocked her to the ground with a great stick. On his arrest Roger insisted he had not meant to hurt Anne and that while he was upstairs looting the house another man, an accomplice, had killed her. Bryant's defence of there being another man with him who was the one to carry out the fatal blow to poor Anne Williams was most likely false as he couldn't name the man and no such person was ever found, but did Roger Bryant deserve the post-mortem punishment of gibbeting when so many murders didn't result in this? From the *Gloucester Journal*:

ROGER BRYANT, indicted for the Murder of ANNE WILLIAMS, on the 3d of April last, by giving her a mortal Wound on the Head, of which she died: TOBIAS LUTON, depos'd, That on Easter Monday he and his wife went to Church, and when they returned, they found Anne Wiliams (their Servant) murder'd, and their House robb'd of a Silver Tankard, two Silver Mugs, a Gold Ring, and Several other things. The Prisoner being a Person of ill Repute was taken up on suspicion of committing the said Murder, &c. but found means to make his escape from the Constable and his Assistants: However, in about three weeks after he was retaken at Cirencester, where he had sold a Ring, which was proved to be Mrs Luton's; and when he was brought to Gloucester he confess'd the Fact to the Persons that guarded him thither, whilst he was at an Inn, and likewise said that he had hid the Plate in a Field near the House from whence he had stolen it; but tho' diligent search was made, yet it could not be found. Upon his Trial, he denied the Fact; but the Evidence being very full against him, he was found guilty of Wilful Murder.
    Sentence of Death. ROGER BRYANT.

ROGER BRYANT order'd for Execution on Wednesday the 9th Instant, near the Place where the Murder was committed, and afterwards to be hang'd in chains there.

Aug 15. Gloucester, Aug 12. On Wednesday last ROGER BRYANT (condemn'd for the Murder of ANNE WILLIAMS, Servnt to Mr LUTON of Doynton, and robbing the House of several Pieces of Plate) was executed on Tug Hill, near the Place where the Murder and Robbery was committed, and afterwards hang'd in chains there. He was about 24 years of age, born of mean Parentage, at Doynton aforesaid, and was put forth Apprentice to a Sheerman, but not liking that Employment, he run away from his Master, and inlisted himself for a Foot Soldier; after which he betook himself to the Business of a Pargiter; and in the latter Part of his Life was a Draoon in the Hon. Brigadier Churchill's Regiment, but deserted. As to the Particulars of the Fact for which he suffered, he said, That having been playing at Skettles on Easter Monday, and Luck running against him, he went to Mr Luton's, thinking to have received a small Matter that was due to him for Work, but Mr Luton and his Wife being gone to Church, he was disappointed: Hereupon he began to tell his Complaint of the Want of Money to an idle Fellow that was begging a draught of Small Beer of the Maid: To which, the Fellow reply'd, D--n it, I believe there is a good Wedge of Money here, let us have it; and accordingly knock'd down the Girl with a great Stick he had in his Hand, and then bid him strike her, which he did; but his Heart failing him, he said, he did not hurt her much; then he went up Stairs and took the Plate mentioned in the Indictment: Bryant added, that whilst he was up Stairs, the other Fellow struck the Maid such a violent Blow, that it made the House shake, (which stroke he believed finish'd her Life) and then made his Escape into a Wood. As he was going to the Place of Execution he discovered where he had hid the Plate, which being found, he had 5 l. given him. 'Tis also very remarkable, that when he came within sight of the House where the Fact was committed he began to be terribly shock'd, and wept bitterly.

Bryant was clearly repentant and much distressed by what he had done. But there was no mercy to be found in this case.

As with all severe punishments, especially capital punishment, there is always the question of doubt. Because gibbeting was such a public spectacle meant to deter other criminals but also to make an example of the hanged man and show everyone in the community what he was, if the sentence turned out to be wrong the damage had very much been done.

The Case of Ely Hatton

Ely Hatton was a poor unfortunate soul. There can be no doubt of that. He was just 24 when he was sentenced to death for the shocking murder of Thomas Turberville. Ely had a poor, unfortunate upbringing, his parents were known to be careless and he was illiterate to the day he died. He lived in Mitcheldean, a small town where he had tried, and failed, to find his way in life. Ely was convicted of this horrific murder, but he protested his innocence right up to the moment he stepped from the ladder and the noose tightened around his young neck. He never confessed.

Mitcheldean is a quiet and detached place today and in 1723 it would have been even more so. Everyone knew everyone and if you were encased in a bad reputation there was no escaping it. Thomas Turberville was a childless widower and lived alone at his shop. Whoever murdered him knew this. Thomas was easy pickings and Ely did know the man; Ely stated that the pair had been out looking for deer to poach that day and even declared his guilt at breaking the sabbath and stating lots of people had to work all week and couldn't take Sundays off. But he insisted he left Thomas alive that day. Thomas died in a brutal and bloody attack that had no clear motive. It wasn't a robbery, though Ely was found to be wearing a shirt that had belonged to Thomas. It was a frenzied attack, and we don't know why. The case against Ely had insufficient evidence to convict him, but when many witnesses came forward to point the finger and there were no other suspects, Ely had to take the fall. As the accounts from the *Gloucester Journal* show, this was a gruesome murder with no known reason and only the most gruesome punishment could fit:

> May 9. Gloucester, May 6. They write from Mitchel Deane in this County, that on Friday the 28th of April last, between the Hours of Seven and Eight in the Evening (as is suppos'd) one THOMAS TURBERVILE of that Town, Carpenter, was in a most barbarous and inhuman Manner murder'd in his own Shop, by having his Brains dash'd out, and afterwards his Skull chopp'd and beat all to Pieces with a broad Axe. The Deceased being a Widower, and having no Child, liv'd alone, and was not found till the Saturday Evening, where the Axe was lying by him all over Gore Blood. The Person

who is justly suspected to have committed this villanous and bloody Fact, is one ELY HATTEN, a weaver, son of Thomas Hatten, of Ruar Deane, Victualler; who was seen between the Hours above mentioned to follow the said Turbervile into his House; and the Deceased was never seen afterwards till found dead in the Manner aforesaid. There are a great many other Circumstances which induce People to believe he was the Person that committed the Fact; one in particular was, that a Shirt and a Pair of Stockings of the Deceased were found on his Back and Legs, when he was under Examination before the Jury at the Inquest. He is now confined in our Castle, and, 'tis to be hop'd, at the next Assizes will meet with as just a Punishment as so desperate and bloody minded a wretch deserves, in order to deter others from committing the like Offence.

Aug 22. Gloucester, Aug 19. Assizes. ELY HATTON, and THOMAS BURCHELL, for Murder; the former for killing Tho. Turbervile, late of Mitchel Dean, Carpenter; and the latter for killing John Causon.

Aug 29. Gloucester, Aug 26. On Wednesday last the Assizes ended here, when one Man received Sentence of Death, viz. ELY HATTON, for the most barbarous and inhuman Murder of Tho. Turbervile, late of Mitchel Dean, Carpenter, on Friday the 28th of April last, who was found in his Shop the next Day with his Brains dash'd out, and his Skull chopp'd to Pieces with a broad Axe, that was lying by him, all over bloody. There were several reputable Witnesses called to prove this horrid Fact, which nothing but ocular Demonstration could tender more plain, for when he was apprehended, he had on a Shirt and a Pair of Stockings of the Deceased's, and his Coat was bloody in several Places. He acknowledged that he was with the Deceased that Evening, and had only to say in Excuse, that the Deceased and he went to a Hill near the Town to view some Deer; but called no body to prove that they were there: He likewise produced no Person to speak to his Reputation, or that could say the least Thing in his Favour: One Man whom he called as a Witness to prove that he saw him about 9 o'clock that Night the Murder was committed, said, he verily believ'd he was the Person that committed the said Murder: In short, no Circumstances ever concurr'd better to prove a Man guilty, than those alleg'd against the Prisoner. One Thing was very remarkable: The Prisoner on his Trial said, the Shirt he had on when apprehended was his Brother's, and on his Examination before the Coroner said it belonged to his Father.

PS. ELY HATTON, we hear, is to be hang'd at Mitchel Dean on Monday the 4th of Sept. Next, and then to be put up in Chains. He is very illiterate, and as yet persists in the Denial of the Fact.

Sep 5. Gloucester, Sep 4. About 7 o'Clock this Morning ELY HATTON, attended by the proper Officers, and a prodigious Concourse of People, was carry'd to Mitchel Dean, in order to be executed near that Place, for the barbarous Murder of THO. TURBERVILE, late of the said Town, Carpenter.

On Monday last ELY HATTON was executed and afterwards hung in Chains on Meane Hill near Mitchel Dean, for the barbarous Murder of Tho. Turbervile, late of that Town, Carpenter. At the Tree he was in a very moving and tender Manner exhorted to confess his Crime, but persisted in the Denial of it to the very Moment that he was turn'd off the Ladder, declaring, as he hop'd for Salvation, he was entirely innocent thereof. He own'd that he had been a great Sabbath Breaker, saying, 'twas usual for young People thereabouts to work all the week, and on the Sunday to go and steal Deer; also that he had been very much addicted to Whoring, which, he said, gave his Conscience the greatest uneasiness. There were near 10,000 spectators present.

Eli Hatton, who was convicted of murder in 1723 and hanged at Pingry Tump at Wigpool overlooking the town, is

said to have cursed the town to plagues of flies! Eli's alleged
victim was Tom Twibervile, a Carpenter who was battered
to death in his shop in the town. Eli's body was hung in a
gibbet, a grim signpost to the town.

The doubt that persisted in this case led many people to think Ely was
innocent, though no such ruling ever came and no other person was ever
found to have committed the murder. If Ely didn't do this and the real
murderer was in the community, or in the vicinity of it, they would have
seen Ely's body hanging in its irons for years to come, a warning, or
perhaps a reminder, that someone else had taken the punishment and the
murderer had got away with it. It may have been hard for Ely's family to
see the gibbet overlooking the town, but it could have given comfort to
a murderer who was never caught.

The Case of William Shaw

In Edinburgh in 1721 William Shaw had rowed bitterly with his daughter
over her choice of husband. William described the man as a brute who
was addicted to every kind of dissipation. William could see this man
was no good for his daughter so he banned the match and instead
chose a much more suitable husband for her. On the evening of their
terrible argument, a neighbour listened in and caught their hurtful words
with some shock. William's daughter, Catherine, talked of her father's
barbarity and cruelty and when William left the house in anger, the
neighbour could hear Catherine moaning as if she was hurt. He went
for help and on entering the house found Catherine dead inside. The
argument the neighbour had heard was enough to have William arrested
and he was later tried and convicted of his daughter's murder. William
Shaw was executed and hanged in chains at Leith Walk. It was almost
a year later when the next inhabitants of the house came across a note
written by Catherine:

BARBAROUS FATHER, —
Your cruelty in having put it out of my power ever to join
my fate to that of the only man I could love, and tyrannically
insisting upon my marrying one whom I always hated, has

25

made me form a resolution to put an end to an existence which is become a burthen to me. I doubt not I shall find mercy in another world; for sure no benevolent being can require that I should any longer live in torment to myself in this! My death I lay to your charge: when you read this, consider yourself as the inhuman wretch that plunged the murderous knife into the bosom of the unhappy CATHERINE SHAW.

William Shaw was innocent. His body and gibbet were swiftly taken down and his remains were passed back to the surviving family for burial. A pair of colours, the national flag and the flag of the regiment William had served in, were waved over his grave as a mark of respect and as recognition of his wrongful conviction.

Women were not usually gibbeted, although there was nothing in law to say they couldn't be. This isn't because women were given special treatment, thought to be too delicate for the practice, or because women didn't commit murder. It was because the female body was so sought after by surgeons, to better understand the complex inner working of this mysterious being, that there were no female criminals left to spare! But even before the Murder Act it's extremely difficult to find a single case of a woman being gibbeted. If there was a sentence of death against a woman she was executed by hanging, or burned at the stake. There may be many reasons why women were not gibbeted, but along with the need for dissection, it's fair to assume that the sight of a female body hanging in chains, inevitably as the weather and birds batter it, a partly naked female body, was thought to be inappropriate and not fit for general viewing. Male bodies seem to have been fair game.

There are some possible exceptions to this, though even if we look further back in history and all over the world, there are very few. In 1664 in Amsterdam, Elsje Christiaens was executed and her body displayed for the murder of her landlady with an axe. Elsje was just 18. There had not been an execution of a woman in Amsterdam for twenty-one years, so it was already of great public interest, and that may have been why authorities chose to display her body as they did. Elsje was first strangled to death, then hit with the axe she had used to murder her landlady and finally her body was hung up on a gibbet post for all to see.

Rembrandt depicted the sight of Elsje's body hanging from the post in his two drawings of the scene. The drawings clearly show Elsje's body suspended from the gibbet post, tied to the post at her calves and under her belly and again, under her arms, making her corpse appear to loll in its lifeless state. This was not a body hung in chains then, but a female murderer displayed on a gibbet post. It's easy to see from the drawings how this looks very much like an evolution of crucifixion.

A more fascinating and compelling case is the one that took place right here in Britain and could be the only woman known to have been hung in chains in this country.

Combe Gibbet in Berkshire today is a replica and has actually been replaced and renewed seven times, such is its importance. It stands 25 ft high on the summit of Inkpen Beacon and is unusual firstly because it is a double gibbet, and secondly because it was reportedly erected for the hanging and gibbeting of one man and one woman. Combe Gibbet was first erected in 1676 and was only used once for its purpose. George Bronman and Dorothy Newman were secret lovers and were arrested for murdering George's wife Martha and their son Robert. The public hanging was to take place on 6 March that year and the pair were to be hung side by side on the gibbet on the hill. The record of the trial is detailed in the Western Circuit Gaol Book for the period 22/23 Charles II, retained in Winchester Library, and astonishingly relays the dispute that arose over who was to pay for the execution, the parish of Combe or Inkpen, which included the cost of two sets of irons. Records then go on to talk of the two dead bodies, post execution, being brought to the Crown and Garter Inn where they were measured by the local blacksmith and then fitted in their 'chaynes'. This is compelling evidence of the only woman known to have been gibbeted in Britain. We always need to take such reports with a pinch of salt as facts have often been massaged and exaggerated, and the story of who was murdered by this pair does change in some reports, but it's hard to argue with written records of two sets of chains and a double gibbet waiting to hang them on. In all other cases where a man and a woman were guilty of murder together, it's clear that although they were both hanged, only the male was gibbeted. Combe Gibbet tells us a different story and for that reason it is an important monument.

The further back we go, the harder it is to haggle with the truth, but in *The Three Centuries of Derbyshire Annals*, there is mention of two men and one woman being gibbeted on Ashover Moor in 1341 for murdering one of the king's purveyors. It's hard to say if this means hanging in chains or whether the use of the word 'gibbet' refers to simple hanging. The wisp of a rumour that a woman was hung in chains is always enticing, though not always reliable.

In 1623 in north Yorkshire, Ralph Raynard – who lived and worked in an inn between the villages of Easingwold and Raskelfe – and his love, Mrs Fletcher, who lived at Thornton Bridge, murdered Mr Fletcher so the pair could be together. They enlisted the help of one Mark Dunn and together the three caught and drowned Mr Fletcher, who knew about his wife's affair and was greatly embarrassed by what was going on. Mr Fletcher was bundled into a sack and sunk in the river. It seems everyone around knew what had been going on between Ralph and Mrs Fletcher and the rumours must have been hot. Although at first the three got away with this, telling anyone who asked that Mr Fletcher had left on account of the rumours, a very clever ploy, eventually Ralph's conscience got the better of him. One night, plagued by nightmares and guilt, he confessed to his sister who was appalled and went quickly to the authorities who arrested and tried Ralph, Mark, and Mrs Fletcher. Reports state the three were executed at Tyburn and their bodies hung in chains near the place of the murder and then their bodies later buried there. The absence of anything stipulating only the two men being hung in chains and Mrs Fletcher suffering a different fate suggests all three were gibbeted, though we don't know this for certain. In *Yorkshire Oddities and Strange Events* by S. Baring Gould, 1900, it says 'about eighty years ago the plough was drawn over the hill when a quantity of bones were unearthed. They were the bones of Raynard, Dunn and Mrs Fletcher'. There is no mention of these bones being found with irons, though it was usual for the irons to be removed when the bones of gibbeted criminals were buried at the site of the gibbet.

The Murder Act was a regulating of how we punished criminals following execution, or what we did with their bodies. Above all things in this Act, it was a way to ensure that murderers and other serious criminals would not be buried – 'in no case whatsoever the body of any murderer shall be suffered to be buried'. They would be either gibbeted or dissected. There's nothing new about insisting criminals were not buried in holy ground or that they should be buried away from the rest of the community, sometimes outside the boundary of that village or town. We've been doing this for as far back as our collective memory knows, and the need to separate murderers from ourselves in the afterlife, or simply to show that 'they' are not with us, not like us, is part of our psyche. The Murder Act, though still pretty vague in some areas, does enforce this. In some cases it seems that for the judge, the decision was black and white. In 1792 at the Thetford assizes in Norfolk, the sitting judge saw two cases of crimes punishable by death, William Anthony for murdering his girlfriend Sarah Cusher, and Richard Burgels for stealing a sheep. Sarah was six months pregnant when William gave her arsenic in the hope of forcing an abortion. Whether he meant to kill the mother as well as the child we don't know, but that was the result. Both Anthony and Burgels had committed crimes punishable by death, but while Anthony had committed murder, Burgels had only stolen a sheep. The judge in this case sentenced both to death, but with the added punishment of hanging in chains for Anthony. Would Anthony have received this harsher punishment if his crime had not been measured against Burgels lesser crime? Though still a terrible crime, Sarah's killing wasn't the usual vicious murder we see resulting in gibbeting. It could have been the existence of the Murder Act that prompted this decision. Both men deserved death, but the Murder Act told the judge that for murder, Anthony should hang in chains as well.

The First Men Gibbeted Under The Murder Act

John Swan was hung in chains on 28 March 1752, just two days after the Murder Act was passed, so it's likely that he was one of the first men to be gibbeted under the terms of the Act.

John Swan became mixed up in a murder plot that he may never have thought of, or carried out, if it wasn't for Elizabeth Jeffries. It's hard to say whether he would have been a murderer, or even a criminal, at all if it wasn't for Elizabeth Jeffries. Elizabeth wanted her uncle dead so she could inherit his estate and after Swan became intimate with her, he believed he was the man to do it. His fate was sealed. The pair tried to enlist a man named Matthews to carry out the actual murder for them, but when he refused it was Swan who shot Mr Jerffries and killed him. The pair were executed and Swan was hung in chains in Epping Forest. There are some conflicting reports about what happened with the placing of the gibbet as one suggests the pair were hanged in the forest and then Swan was moved to another part of the forest to be gibbeted, but it seems that Swan's gibbet was relocated on account of it being in view of some gentlemen's houses. After some consideration it was found that a better place for the gibbet would be Bucket's Hill near the Bald Faced Stag Inn. The reasons for this seem bizarre as the *General Advertiser* states, 'the Bald Faced Stag, was a proper place, not only in situation, but it being a place where Mr Jeffreys [the victim] often resorted from whence Swan used to fetch him.' The placing of a gibbet near a favoured place of the victim, and that connected the victim with the murderer, is unusual and suggests some level of sentimentality not often heard of when considering locations for gibbets.

James Stewart

In May of 1752 James Stewart was convicted of a murder committed near Appin in the Scottish West Highlands. It was a complex time in Scottish history, with tensions still high following the Jacobite rebellion. Colin Campbell was a government appointed factor who would take possession of goods on behalf of others, in this case the government, and as such he was on his way to evict Stewart tenants from their properties when he was shot in the back. His companion, Mungo Campbell, was only able to give a very vague description of the gunman, but James Stewart was swiftly arrested based on the fact that he and Campbell had been known to quarrel and had a dislike for each other. James Stewart was to be sentenced for the murder, even though there was no real evidence against him. These were tense times and someone had to take the fall. James Stewart maintained his innocence and he certainly wasn't short of supporters, but he was still sentenced to death and to be hung in chains as a warning to others. His body hung in chains for eighteen months, after which time his remains were secretly taken down and buried in the Chapel of Kells, an eleventh-century chapel in Argyll and Bute. The authorities walked a dicey line in this case. They needed to make an example of someone for this murder amid such difficult unrest, but by doing so they also bolstered the supporters on Stewart's side. This is perhaps why he only hung in chains for a short time and no effort was made to uncover who removed him and gave him his proper burial.

The Tale of Gatward's Gibbet

A Cambridgeshire antiquarian, William Cole, wrote of a gibbeting that took place on Caxton Gibbet, a small hill between London and Huntington. In 1753 the son of a Mrs Gatward was convicted of robbing the mail, a very serious crime at the time. He was executed and hung in chains on the great road. William Cole wrote that he had seen the body of young Gatward hanging there for between two and four months and that the man was wearing a scarlet coat in his gibbet. It was thought a screw that supported the gibbet had been filed and the gibbet fell from its post in the high winds. Family members often attempted to remove the gibbet and bury their loved ones in secret and members of the community may have had some sympathy for the defendant, as he was not a murderer. The idea that gibbeting prevented the soul from passing over, due to the body not being buried whole, could even have caused the local blacksmith himself to sabotage the gibbet he created.

It's worth putting gibbeting into perspective. While it's true that we did execute people for things that would seem fairly petty today – stealing a horse was punishable by death – gibbeting was actually comparatively rare. Between the years of 1752, when the Murder Act came into force, and 1832, when the Anatomy Act was introduced, only 13 per cent of criminals sentenced to death were gibbeted. So, while there is no doubt that we were a much more bloodthirsty society and we did bestow some pretty horrendous punishments on criminals, we weren't hanging criminals in chains at every corner of the road. Following the Murder Act, gibbeting actually appears to have lessened. Perhaps, as with most things, once legislation is put into place to say this is to be done, people lose their taste for it. It is no longer a lawless practice, but something stipulated by an Act of Parliament. We can see how few and far between gibbeting becomes once the Act has been passed, in contrast to how frequent and random it seems to have been before.

In 1770, highwayman Robert Haslett was the first man to be gibbeted in the North East following the introduction of the Murder Act. This area of England had passed eighteen years without a single gibbeting taking place – testament to how rare gibbeting actually was. However, Robert Haslett changed all that when he robbed the mail on the Gateshead Fell. *The Gentleman's Magazine* recorded at the time that Haslett's body was hanged for two hours before it was taken down and carried in a cart to the gibbet, which had been erected on the east side of the Durham Road. There he was hung in chains and left to rot. In 1772 the Reverend James Murray passed the gibbet on the road and lamented on its cruelty. Had Robert Haslett simply stolen from individuals, he remarked, he wouldn't have suffered such a fate, but because he chose to rob the mail, this horrendous practice was visited on his lifeless body. In 1776 a travelling Quaker stated that he passed Haslett's body still in its gibbet and that he seemed to be perfectly intact.

Although the Murder Act puts into law a practice that had been taking place for centuries before and gave only two options for dealing with the remains of murderers, it didn't make clear which punishment should be used in which cases. It was still the decision of the authorities in each community whether to hang in chains or to dissect, and more often than not they chose to dissect. This could have been because of the cost involved in gibbeting, the issue of where to place them in communities and also the need to reserve this extra punishment for very serious crimes. In some cases, we see that the sentence is first dissection and is then later changed to hanging in chains. From the *London Chronicle*:

> 1763
>
> Mar 14. Our Assizes were concluded on Saturday morning; at which THOMAS HANKS, of Wick Rissington, for the murder of his wife, was the only person capitally convicted. The trial of this man lasted seven hours, and during the course of it there appeared such a combination of concurrent circumstances as fully evidenced his guilt. The pathetick eloquence of Mr Justice WILMOT, in his admonition to the unhappy convict, was beyond conception great; but the prisoner's obdurate insensibility was observed with concern by the whole court; for after sentence was pronounced against him, he said, I am an innocent man; in which declaration he still persists. His body was at first ordered to be dissected, but the sentence is since changed, and he is to be hanged in chains near the scene of that horrid fact. He will be executed this day. His mother, charged as being accessary to the murder, was acquitted.

> Mar 21. On Monday last THOMAS HANKS was executed here, agreeable to his sentence. His behavioiur was expressive of the deepest penitence for the sins of his past life, but he persevered in denying the murder for which he suffered.

In this case it seems to have been Hanks's refusal to confess and show repentance that led to the change in the sentence. Ironic then, that he may have received a more brutal punishment because he did not commit the crime and declined to say he did.

Frank Fearne of Sheffield is another example of a sentence being changed. In 1782, Fearne enticed a watchmaker, Nathan Andrews, onto open and barren ground on the outskirts of the city at Loxley on the pretence of taking him to sell a watch at a watch club. Fearne had elaborated this lie so he could have the watch for himself and in taking it, he viciously stabbed Andrews a number of times and not being satisfied with that, beat his skull in with a hedge stake. He left Andrews's body there until it was discovered by some other person walking by. Fearne had been seen with Andrews earlier that evening, so he was soon arrested for the murder. The judge in this case first sentenced Fearne to execution and then dissection, but after further thought changed his mind. An order for the alteration of the specifics of the punishment was sent to the governor of York Castle where Fearne was executed. From *Criminal Chronology of York Castle 1867*:

> I do hereby order that the execution of Francis Fearne be respited until Tuesday 23rd of July and that his body [instead of being anatomised] shall be afterwards hanged in chains on a gibbet, to be erected on some conspicuous spot, on Loxley Common in the parish of Ecclesfield, in the county of York, at a convenient distance from the highway.

Fearne's body was brought from York in its irons and the post was erected on Loxley common, where it remained for twenty-five years.

It may have been a simple case of the judge realising, after the fact, how brutal this murder was, or more likely, he felt some pressure from members of the community or perhaps Andrews's family, to inflict further lasting punishment on Fearne's body. With the Murder Act now placing gibbeting in law, it was both something the judge could order and perhaps something he thought he should order. There are some cases where the judge wouldn't have been left with an option, however, as surgeons did sometimes refuse the bodies for dissection. If this was the body of a murderer, hanging in chains would have then been the only possibility left.

In 1759 *The London General Evening Post* describes the strange case of Robert Saxby. Robert was 72 and a grandfather from Surrey. He murdered his brother's wife in cold blood. The newspaper report states that Robert was unrepentant and confessed the crime, saying he would have done it sooner, but didn't find the opportunity before. The reason given was that 'the deceased took more notice of a grandchild than she took of his son'. It seems a strange reason and it's unclear whether this means Robert Saxby's son the poor woman wasn't paying enough attention to or her own. Either way, a bizarre motive for murder! He was executed in August at Guildford and apparently, seemingly uncaring of the fact, said he wouldn't have lived much longer anyway if this 'hadn't happened'. Robert's body, 72 at the time of his execution, was sent to the surgeons for dissection. It's likely the judge in this case would have felt this to be the better option. Robert was an old man and despite his crime, gibbeting may have felt unsavoury. However, the surgeons didn't want him either, and they refused to dissect the body on account of it being 'too old'. Robert Saxby was sent back from the surgeons, leaving only one other option for the judge. His body was hung in chains at Wootton where the crime had taken place.

Chapter 2

The Making of a Gibbet

Despite place names and some roads still holding onto the ghost of this gruesome practice, gibbeting did not have a specific location and gibbets were not erected in one particular place. Gibbet Moor, Gibbet Lane and even The Noose and Gibbet Inn, all suggest these were sites of regular gibbeting and these places were reserved for this practice, but that wasn't the case. Although there are some exceptions to this, one being mentioned above – Caxton Gibbet, the scene of that supposed horrific live gibbeting following the murder of the man named Partridge, was also the place where, following the introduction of the Murder Act, young Gatward was gibbeted for robbing the mail. These two sperate crimes and punishments could have been held in this same place by coincidence, or it may have been known as Caxton Gibbet already, following the earlier incident. But this is unusual. Gibbets were erected as close to the scene of the crime as possible, so a stretch of moorland nearby, a prominent hill, or a lane by a murder, were the chosen places to gibbet the criminal. As gibbets were erected and used per crime, and in most cases never used to gibbet anyone else, these sites are the locations of specific gibbetings.

Other Exceptions

In 1603 William Pendleton murdered John Young. He was executed and hung in chains on Barmby Moor, Yorkshire. In 1659 Charles Spooner from Bradford robbed and murdered Francis Groves. He was executed at St Leonard's Green, Green Dykes, York, and hung in chains on Barmby Moor. It's unclear if both of these murders, or either of them, took place at Barmby. William Pendleton was from nearby Pocklington and reports suggest the murder of Francis Groves took place at Barmby Moor, but it could also have been a location deemed ideal for the gibbet. If both murders took place in the area the moor may have been chosen for its drastic effect. Viewing the gibbet from the road as it swung up on the moor would have created more terror. For the second gibbeting, the moor would have still held the memory of the first so could have been chosen with that in mind also.

In 1774 in the West Riding of Yorkshire Thomas Spencer approached Robert Thomas and Matthew Normanton and offered to pay them to commit a murder for him. Spencer wanted Mr Deighton dead, but he didn't want to get his own hands dirty. The pair agreed to carry out the kill for Spencer and in the spring of that year Normanton fired the shot that ended Deighton's life. When the pair were arrested Thomas quickly confessed to his part in the crime, named Spencer, and explained that Normanton had fired the shot. But Normanton had escaped and in August of that year it was Thomas who was executed and hung in chains on Beacon Hill, Halifax. Legend says his hand was fixed so it pointed to where the crime had taken place. Matthew Normanton was caught in April of the following year, also executed, and taken in his irons to hang with his accomplice, now rotting, on Beacon Hill. Thomas Spencer got away with his part in this murder, but in 1783 his crimes began to catch up with him when he was arrested for inciting a grain riot. Years earlier Spencer had also been one of the coiners of Cragg Vale, a famous group of counterfeiters. He had organised and paid for a murder and had counterfeited the coin, but he was eventually executed for rioting and stealing grain. Spencer was publicly hung on a purposefully constructed gallows on Beacon Hill. We don't know if Robert Thomas or Matthew Normanton's bodies still stood in their gibbets at this time, but even if they didn't the memory of this distasteful site would still have held in the minds of the many onlookers who came to watch Spencer hang that day. It seems like rough justice, especially for Robert Thomas, but after hanging for the appropriate amount of time, career criminal Thomas Spencer was returned to his family and buried in holy ground at Heptonstall churchyard.

Peter's Stone, Gibbet Rock, The Peak District

We do know that Anthony Lingard, the last man gibbeted in Derbyshire, was hung in chains on this limestone dome at Wardlow Mires in the Peak

District. The dome rises in front of you as you make your way along this country trail and it must have been an eerie spectacle to travel along here and be confronted with the site of the corpse swinging in its gibbet cage up atop this high dome on the hill. Whether this dome was already called Gibbet Rock we don't know, but we do know Lingard wasn't the first man to be hung at this location. Years earlier, Black Harry the highwayman was also gibbeted on Peter's Stone, close to the routes he had used to rob passing travellers. The site of the highwayman hanging up on the rock would have been gruesome enough and it's doubtful it made anyone feel any safer while passing through this area.

Blockhouse Point

In 1776 naval seaman Francis Arsine murdered Peter Varley by stabbing him to death at Blockhouse Point, Portsmouth. He was executed and hung in chains on the very spot. In 1777 Jack the painter was executed and also hung on a gibbet at Blockhouse Point. Jack the painter, so called because he had been an apprentice painter, was born James Hill in Edinburgh, but through his criminal escapades went by various aliases. He was caught for burning down the centre for the Royal Navy at Portsmouth. He was executed and gibbeted at Blockhouse Point. In 1781 John Bryan was sentenced to death for murder and was gibbeted close to the gibbet of the now infamous Jack the painter, at Blockhouse Point. Blockhouse Point is one of only a few cases of locations becoming known for gibbetings. This was usually because the locations were used for certain crimes, a prominent spot at the docks was seen as perfect for gibbeting pirates as it would be seen by many other pirates. But the collecting of bodies in one place like this would have intensified the terrible smell of rotting flesh and the macabre spectacle of corpses swinging together in the sea breeze. It's hard to imagine how people who lived or worked close to this, or even just passed through, ever got used to it.

Coincidence or Convenience?

There is just one case known of two murderers who were hanged on the same day at the same place and then transported that same day to the scenes of their crimes, just 23 miles apart, to be hung in chains. Because gibbeting was so rare in each county this is a very unusual occurrence and is either a strange coincidence, or the result of a judge faced with two murderers and being unable to separate their crimes. The year was 1795 and the two men were Stephen Watson and Henry Bennington.

Henry Bennington murdered his employer, John Filbee. Why he did this is lost to time, but he was arrested and sentenced for the murder. At the same time the Thetford assizes were dealing with the case of Stephen Watson who murdered his wife Elizabeth. This is said to have been an unprovoked and shocking attack. The two men were tried at the same time and both received the death penalty. Unusually, they were both executed at Thetford gaol and not at Norwich Castle. There had been some debate and complaints about the use of Thetford gaol for executions and it is recorded as only being used in 1795, and then each year until 1801. The complaints centred around the executions causing the gaoler to be absent from the gaol for a number of days. The court and gaol were a quarter of a mile apart and the reason for the absence, and subsequent security risk and of leaving prisoners unattended to for days on end, is unknown. The two prisoners were both executed on 25 March 1795. As they were both to be hung in chains back at the scenes of their crimes 23 miles apart, we presume the blacksmiths from each community travelled to the gaol to measure them and fit their irons. We don't know of any other instance where this happened. Gibbeting was so infrequent, did the blacksmiths each make up their own irons or did they have occasion to consult each other on this? Or was it the same blacksmith for both? The men were then transported to the place of their gibbetings. We can only imagine what the atmosphere around this would have been like. Gibbetings attracted great crowds and with such a short distance between the two being gibbeted at the same time, it must have felt like a festival of the gibbet!

The making of a gibbet was a speedy process, because it had to be. Following the execution of the criminal his gibbet was usually made available the same day and the body was transported to it. A hanged man would be left in his noose for around an hour, sometimes more. This was to be certain that the person was indeed dead before he was taken down, though even after this time there are cases of the hanged man still being alive when removed from his noose. This also gave authorities the time to clear away the vast crowds that often congregated at public hangings.

The body was then taken away to be fitted into the irons. There are some reports that talk of the body being 'tarred' at this point, but it's uncertain if this was a regular practice or not. Tarring was presumably done to help preserve the body a little longer while it decayed in its irons, prolonging the spectacle of the corpse hanging on its gibbet before it rotted away. In some cases it was a week between the hanging of the criminal and the hanging in chains, and this was most likely due to the time it took to construct the particular gibbet and the time to transport the body from the place of hanging back to the scene of the crime. In some cases the location of execution was many miles from the desired site of the gibbet, which was as close to the crime as possible. Before the introduction of the Murder Act, hangings and gibbetings did often take place at the same location – the scene of the crime – but as hangings gravitated to the gaol where the prisoner was held, the need to transport the body to the place of gibbeting caused a delay between the two practices. Authorities usually preferred to execute criminals as soon as possible following sentencing, the next day, or within two days. Usually they would have been measured by the blacksmith for their gibbet irons already, so that they could be hung in chains immediately after execution, but sometimes that wasn't possible. In the case of John Barchard, his post-execution body was taken from Norwich Castle back to the scene of his crime, but was then taken back to the castle gaol for his irons to be re-sized, suggesting they were made hastily following his execution and didn't fit him properly. The worst part of the process for the criminal would have been between sentencing and execution and sometimes this was stretched unbearably. As prisoners waited in their damp, dark cells for the day of their hanging to arrive, they often wrote letters to loved ones, gave full confessions to the priest, and contemplated what they had done. It could be said that this time of waiting for their public death was the worst punishment of all.

The Case of Tom Colley

Times were hard in rural Gubblecote, Hertfordshire, in 1751, and for Ruth and John Osborn things were desperate. The husband and wife were poor and spent their days begging for scraps of food from anyone they came across. One day Ruth walked to John Butterfields's farm in Gubblecoate, where she saw pales of buttermilk standing full to the brim. She asked John if he could spare some of the copious amounts of buttermilk, but the farmer replied that the milk was for his hogs and he wouldn't give her any. Affronted and starving, Ruth called him selfish and left. Soon after this John Butterfield suffered a fit and his calves became ill. Rather than seeing this as unfortunate and bad luck, the farmer was convinced Ruth had cursed him and that she was a witch. Despite the practice of ducking witches being outlawed by then, this community demanded an old-fashioned witch trial by drowning and the town criers in Leighton Buzzard and Hemel Hemstaed apparently announced the ducking of Ruth and John Osborn, suspected witches. This is where Tom Colley comes in.

Colley was a chimney sweep and the one tasked with prodding and turning the suspects while they were dunked under the water attached to a ducking stool. The experience would have been humiliating, terrifying, and was ultimately fatal for the Osborns. They were wrapped in sheets and their hands and feet tied while they were ducked in a nearby pond. They didn't stand a chance. Thomas Colley was revered for his part in the ducking by the community and even collected money from parishioners for saving them from the witch and seeing to it that they received the proper justice. However, this practice was illegal and it wasn't long before the authorities heard of it. Colley was arrested for murder, found guilty, and sentenced to death, though in his community he was still considered a martyr. Thomas was executed and hung in chains close to the scene of the crime. Although Colley was tried and sentenced on 29 July 1751, he wasn't executed and gibbeted until 24 August. The time in between was unusual, but was most likely due to preparations having to be made for the gibbet. Execution was quick and easy, but uncommonly, constructing the gibbet was not. In gaol, awaiting his punishment, Colley wrote a full confession. It's impossible to know whether he was persuaded to do this, or if the realisation of his fate made him remorseful.

The confession:

> Good People I beseech you all to take Warning, by an Unhappy Man's Suffering, that you be not deluded into so absurd & wicked a Conceit, as to believe that there are any such Beings upon Earth as Witches.

It was that Foolish and vain Imagination, heightened and inflamed by the strength of Liquor, which prompted me to be instrumental (with others as mad-brained as myself) in the horrid & barbarous murther of Ruth Osborn, the supposed Witch; for which I am now so deservedly to suffer Death.

I am fully convinced of my former Error and with the sincerity of a dying Man declare that I do not believe there is such a Thing in Being as a Witch: and I pray God that none of you thro' a contrary Persuasion, may hereafter be induced to think that you have a Right in any shape to persecute, much less endanger the Life of a Fellow-Creature.

I beg of you all to pray to God to forgive me & to wash clean my polluted Soul in the Blood of Jesus Christ my Saviour & Redeemer.

So Exhorteth you all the Dying
Thomas Colley
Signed at Hertford August 23rd 1751

Thomas Colley's ghost is said to roam Gubblecoate in the form of a black dog with yellow fangs.

It was the responsibility of the county sheriff to oversee all this and it was often a difficult and costly exercise. Local blacksmiths were employed to make the iron cage, but it was unlikely they had ever been called upon to do this before, so in many cases they didn't have any prior knowledge of what a gibbet cage looked like and they had to make it up anew each time. This is why no two gibbets look the same. The cost involved is most likely the overriding reason why the practice was carried out rarely. Although it was still cheaper than holding prisoners in gaol for long periods of time, it was a hefty cost for any sheriff to have to justify and cover.

In the case of George Bronman and Dorothy Newman mentioned earlier, the argument about which parish should pay for the erection of the gibbet post and the chains the pair were to be hung in shows how significant these costs were. While George was from Combe, Dorothy was from Inkpen and the dispute centred around where the gibbet should be erected and most importantly, who would bear the cost. In the end the gibbet was erected on the boundary and the two parishes shared the cost, but they would both have still felt the pinch tightly. Erecting a gibbet and creating custom made chains for murderers wasn't cheap.

The costs of constructing and erecting a gibbet and gibbet cage vary wildly from year to year and place to place. From £9 for the gibbeting of Francis Jennison in Hampshire in 1794 to £25 for gibbeting William Jones in Hertfordshire just four years earlier in 1790. It's not clear why there are such huge jumps in the costing, but location and transporting of bodies must have come into play. The cost would have included the blacksmith's fee for making the irons themselves, plus the gibbet post which had to be constructed so it was sturdy enough to hold the hanging irons for many years, and also secure enough to ensure no one could dismantle it.

The word 'gibbet' was originally used to describe the entire structure, the scaffolding and the post included, and there is some confusion in historical texts and stories as to whether prisoners were hung in chains or simply hung from the gibbet post as execution. There are many mentions of gibbets in Shakespeare, but it seems this was in reference to hangings and the gallows in general. In Halifax, the Halifax Gibbet, a popular tourist attraction on Gibbet Street, is in fact an early guillotine and not a post for hanging prisoners in chains. But by the eighteenth century the word was more commonly used to describe the body cage specifically.

The making of the gibbet may have been costly and difficult, and gibbets made to last, but that didn't stop members of the community and the murderer's family from trying to dismantle them. Authorities were well aware of the threat of gibbets being taken down so families could bury their loved ones, or collectors and tourists bagging a souvenir, and it was stipulated in a clause in the Murder Act that any attempt to do this was unlawful. The sentence if caught was transportation for seven years. Still, gibbets were tampered with and bodies stolen from time to time. There doesn't, however, seem to be any records of anyone being prosecuted for doing this. When bodies were stolen from gibbets it's recorded that the culprits, and usually the bodies, were never found, and in some cases it seems a blind eye was turned. Still, attempting to steal bodies from the gibbet was a risky business and the fear of what would happen to you if you were caught was real.

The Case of William Jobling

On 1 August 1832 in Durham, William Jobling was found guilty of the murder of Nicholas Fairles, a 71-year-old magistrate who Jobling and his fellow drinker, Ralph Armstrong, had beaten to death. Despite Fairles himself stating Armstrong was the principal attacker before he died, the man was never seen again and it was Jobling who took the rap. His sentence was to be hanged two days later on 3 August and to be then hung in chains as close to the scene of the murder as possible. Although William denied being the person who delivered the fatal blow to Fairles, he accepted his sentence, he prayed while awaiting his punishment and asked that his great sorrow at what had happened be passed onto the family of Nicholas Fairles, and that they might forgive him for his part in the death.

It's said that William was brave as he faced his execution, but he was unable to speak and deliver the address he had intended to give to the onlookers. William's body hung for an hour before it was cut down and transported back to the gaol where it remained while the gibbet was made ready. The gibbet should be ready on the same day as execution, but the sheriff and a blacksmith had been given just two days to construct and erect the said gibbet, and this proved too arduous a task for them, meaning there was a delay. It was a wet day on 3 August and not as many people as expected had turned out to watch this ghoulish spectacle, but still fifty foot-soldiers stood between the hangman's drop and the small crowd, and were then on hand to take the body back to Jarrow Slake, where the crime had been committed. Once William's body was back at the gaol his clothes were removed, he was covered in tar, and his clothes were then replaced. It was then a further three days before the gibbet was ready, and William's tarred and lifeless body was forced to wait at the gaol. At seven o clock on Monday morning he was taken on a wagon drawn by two horses and escorted by a troop of hussars, two companies of infantry, the sheriff, the bailiff, the gaoler, and officers of the gaol, from Durham to Jarrow Slake. They arrived at half past one. Again, spectators were notably few and the body was placed in flat irons of 2½ in wide. The feet were in stirrups and at each side of the head were bars that met above him in a ring from which the whole thing was suspended. A bar ran down the middle of the back and also down the breast, and bars ran the inside of the legs. The circular iron at the throat kept the head from lolling and subsequently William appeared to be gazing up towards the sky, and perhaps heaven. A 1½ ton weight was sunk in the slake and the gibbet structure was fixed in stone. The timber was 21 ft high and iron bars were attached at either side to prevent anyone from sawing it down.

43

The gibbet stood in place opposite the scene of the murder. On the night of 31 August in the deepest dark hours, William Jobling's body was removed from the gibbet and taken away secretly. It was never found. Who did this, or where Jobling's body was buried, remained a mystery, but it's clear the appetite for this practice was wearing thin by this time. William Jobling was the last man to be gibbeted in the North East.

An Attempt to Bury the Bodies

The following two cases from the Gloucester Journals describe four men to be hung in chains simultaneously, though not at the same location. This is two separate cases of murder, both including the two men involved being sentenced to be hung in chains, very unusual for one county. Interestingly, Thomas Cambrey, who protested his innocence, went unbelieved by the community and seems to have been treated with further contempt for his refusal to confess, while Henry Payne and Andrew Burnett admitted their guilt and were said to be very repentant, and so received much more forgiveness. An attempt was made to take their bodies down and bury them, unsuccessfully, presumably by their families. As their bodies were discovered 'among the Rocks', we can only presume they were disturbed in the act and knowing what they were doing was illegal, abandoned their attempts. The rotting bodies were then taken and once again placed in their gibbet irons.

> Gloucester, Nov 5. Last Wednesday, THOMAS CAMBREY, of Cirencester, Saltman, and JOHN CURTIS, Labourer, were committed to our Castle Gaol, being charg'd on the Oaths of THOMAS STEPTOE (their Accomplice) and ESTHER ILES, with breaking into the House of JAMES MILLINGTON, in the Parish of Cirencester aforesaid, on the 25th of October last, and robbing the same of Money, &c. To the value of 20 l. And upwards; and also with wounding the said MILLINGTON, his Wife and Daughter; of which Wounds his said Wife is since dead.

> Dec 27. Gloucester, Dec 24. Last Tuesday ANDREW BURNET and HENRY PAIN, two foot Soldiers, were

brought from Bristol, to our Castle, for the Murder of RICHARD RUDDLE, late Coachman to Sir ROBERT CANN, Bart. and robbing him of his Watch, &c. which Watch was found in the Possession of the said BURNET.

Mar 6. Gloucester, Mar 3. THOMAS CAMBREY and JOHN CURTIS, for breaking into the House of JAMES MILLINGTON, and robbing the same of Money, &c. To the Value of 20 l. And for killing the said MILLINGTON's Wife.

Mar 13. Gloucester, Mar 10. Trial and condemnation of THOMAS CAMBREY and JOHN CURTIS; also ANDREW BURNET and HENRY PAYNE.
Gloucester, Mar 12. Yesterday about One o'clock in the Morning, JOHN CURTIS died in the Condemn'd Room

Mar 20. Gloucester, Mar 17. THOMAS CAMBREY, condemn'd at our last Assizes for the Murder of JAMES MILLINGTON's Wife, and robbing his House, has, since the Death of his Accomplice, JOHN CURTIS, been very ill, but is now much better, and is to be executed on Tuesday next, near the Bowling Green House at Cirencester, and afterwards to be hung up in Chains: He denies both the said Crimes. As he has been ill, the Under Sheriff intends to take him, HENRY PAYNE, and ANDREW BURNET, in a Coach to Cirencester. And on Wednesday Morning sets out with the two latter for Tetbury, Didmarton, Petty France, Sodbury and Bristol; and they are to be executed on Thursday at Durdham Down, where they robbed and murdered Sir ROBERT CANN's Coachman; and afterwards to be hung up in Chains on Horvill Green. They are very penitent, and confess the Robbery; but say they had no Intent to have committed the Murder.

Mar 27. Gloucester, Mar 24. We have an Account from Cirencester, that on Tuesday last, at the Execution of THOMAS CAMBREY, for the Murder of Mrs MILLINGTON, &c. There was the greatest Number of People ever seen on such an Occasion: He deny'd the Fact; and also declared, that he never saw CURTIS till they were sent to Gaol together; upon which one of the Spectators said to him, How can you die with such a Lie in your Mouth! I have seen you several Times drinking together. He was afterwards hung in chains.

And on Thursday, HENRY PAYNE and ANDREW BURNET were executed at Durdham Down, on the Rocks, above the Hot Well: They were both very penitent, and own'd the Robbery and Murder of Sir ROBERT CANN's Coachman, tho' they said it was not their Intent to have kill'd him; but he being a Stout resolute Man, BURNET gave him the unhappy Blow that occasion'd his Death. They are likewise in Chains.

May 1. Bristol, Apr 28. Last Friday Night the bodies of HENRY PAYNE, and ANDREW BURNET, (who were executed for the Murder of Sir ROBERT CANN's Coachman) were stolen off the Gibbet on Durdham Down; but have since been found among the Rocks, and hung up again.

It seems John Curtis and Thomas Cambrey both fell very ill following their sentencing, with Curtis actually dying before he faced his fate of hanging. Since Cambrey continued to protest his innocence right to the last, there has to be some doubt about what happened. Cambrey even said he didn't know the now dead Curtis. As this was rubbished by witnesses who said he drank with the man, it's hard to unpick this story and find the truth of what happened. We don't know if it was Mr Millington who named them following the murder of his wife in the burglary, or if the arrest came about by other means, but it is stated that their accomplice, Thomas Steptoe, gave testimony against them. Perhaps he saw his chance to pass blame. Whatever happened, it's a sad and sorry tale, and perhaps proof of the immense stress and horror the prospect of hanging and gibbeting did strike in these men as they awaited the gallows and the irons.

Kenneth Leal

In 1773 in Elgin, Scotland, Kenneth Leal was executed and hung in chains for robbing the mail. Some reports say his body was stolen from the gibbet, but following a flood in the area in 1829, workmen uncovered his body at the site where the gibbet had stood, still intact in its gibbet cage. To have stolen the body and buried it at the site seems unlikely, and we do know that the bodies of gibbeted criminals were, after a period of time, taken down and their remains buried at the foot of the gibbet without ceremony or a marked grave. To find remains still in the cage and the irons intact is remarkable and a report from the *Elgin Courant* in 1868 gives us a detailed description of the gibbet found by the workmen:

> The chain was first got hold of and on pulling it up all the hoops attached to it and encircling the body were brought to light. The complete apparatus consisted of a ring round each ankle, from which a chain of ordinary make passed up either leg and was fastened to a band of strong hoop iron round the body; from this ring or band four straps of a similar construction passed over the shoulders to the ring that encircled the neck, the neck ring in its turn being attached to the head cap, which consisted of four straps passing up either side of the head and meeting at the top where a strong swivel link was rivetted through them to allow it to turn with the wind. The body was suspended from the gibbet by a chain rather more than two feet long and made of three-eights of an inch round iron, the links being about three inches in diameter, in the form of a common chimney 'crook'. The bones and the whole apparatus were again buried, with the exception of the head piece and the chain to which it was rivetted; these were carried as trophies to Longhill and hung dangling on the garde paling near Mr Sellars's workshop.

From this and the description of Jobling's irons above, we can see how different each gibbet was. Blacksmiths were essentially measuring a man's body and then making up a construction that they thought would best do the job. There were no plans or earlier descriptions to work with. But whatever exact form the gibbet irons took, however it was intricately constructed, it was essentially the same thing. It was a body shaped cage, made to hold a dead body while it hung between earth and heaven, on display and decaying in the wind and rain. From gibbets preserved in museums today we can see how different they were. John Keale's irons on display in Louth Museum are for the head and torso only. The cage opens with hinges and was closed and bolted around the corpse. The gibbet on display at Nottingham Museum of Crime and Justice, thought to be that of James Cook, is a full body gibbet with leg and arm irons also, as most appear to have been. Surviving head irons are also very different. If we compare Tom Otter's head irons on display at Doddington Hall with Ralph Smith's head irons at the Boston Guildhall Museum, there are some clear differences. Otter's head irons are much sturdier. The flat irons that fit around the skull are wider and the neck brace is much thicker with chunky bolts. There is also an iron rod protruding down at the front of the irons which may have fitted at the nose of the skull. In stark comparison Ralph Smith's irons appear much lighter. The neck brace is markedly smaller and the bolts more delicate. Although these irons are clearly incomplete now, the difference is startling. Ralph Smith's head irons are also much smaller in size than Tom Otter's, suggesting he was a smaller man. Perhaps Tom Otter's size made the blacksmith feel they needed to make the irons heavy, but as each gibbet was made up by blacksmiths with no instructions, it could also have been an over-eager iron maker. Gervase Matcham's waist belt from his gibbet cage is on display at the Norris Museum in Cambridgeshire and the description on this item tells us in detail how this was made and how it worked, 'a belt in five hinged sections joined at the front with a knob fitting into a keyhole, and with smaller holes round the belt for the attachment of chains etc. Width 65mm, length about 100cms.' This helps us to see how the irons were attached to the corpse after execution. The contraption was hinged at all points so it could be fitted around a dead body and secured there. Stephen Watson's gibbet, now displayed at Norwich Castle, has only survived partially, but is clearly different from other discovered irons, as the information for the cage tells us:

> Norwich Castle Museum holds a substantial part of the gibbet cage of Stephen Watson, which was uncovered on Bradenham Common by H. Rider Haggard in 1899. Although affected by rust, the surviving portion of the gibbet comprises a headpiece with four vertical straps, one of which must have covered part of the face. There is a torso consisting of vertical bars which are continuation of

the head piece, and much less substantial horizontal bands which have largely not survived except around the places where they attach to the vertical bars. There is evidence that the horizontal straps were punched several times to be adjustable. No arm or leg pieces survive although a rivet hole in the gusset suggests that leg piece formerly were attached there. The swivel eye shows considerable wear. Associated with this gibbet cage are two skull fragments.

This also tells us, again, that the skull was often the only part of the skeleton remaining in the irons when the relic was found.

Some records suggest that it was the sight of the chains that affected the prisoner more than the gallows, and Ralph Smith is said to have only lost his composure when being measured for his irons. The thought of their own bodies hanging in the gibbet, exposed to the elements, for years to come without the prospect of a proper burial, caused hardened criminals to falter in their emotional control.

Career Criminals and the Fear of the Gibbet

When career criminal William Lewin was awaiting his punishment in Chester Castle in 1791 he enquired what would happen to his body after he was hanged. The pamphlet 'The Trail of William Lewin' published soon after his death tells us 'Soon after condemnation he was very defirous to know what they intended to do with his body; when told he was to be gibbetted, he feemed more affected than had ever been obferved before.' Lambert Reading was a career criminal and part of a gang of prolific housebreakers and robbers. It's unclear if there was any violence to speak of involved in these burglaries, but when Lambert was eventually caught in 1775 and convicted of burglary he was sentenced to death, and to be hung in chains. To impose such an extreme punishment for something other than murder following the Murder Act is highly unusual – for the crime and for the year – and it did have an unusual effect on Lambert. The *Scots Magazine* issue 37, reports 'part of his sentence was to be hung in chains, a matter which brought him to some reflection and was the first circumstance which seemed to touch his sensibility'. He was 'exceedingly shocked and begged to be allowed a burial.'

At this point the authorities were able to strike a deal with Lambert. He gave them information on the gang's plans for further housebreaking and arson, and his sentence was altered to mere execution to be followed by burial. Was gibbeting simply a threat to get Lambert to talk? Or were the authorities really going to hang one man from this gang in chains for simple housebreaking? As a threat it certainly did the trick, which leads us to wonder, was the prospect of gibbeting known to cause such reactions in hardened criminals? The notorious pirate John Gow endured with discipline the torture performed on him in the hope of procuring a confession. But when it was expressed to him that he would be gibbeted he soon gave in. Albert Hartshorne's book *Hanging in Chains* published in 1891 described Gow as saying, 'he would not have given so much trouble if he could have been assured of not being hung in chains. He was convicted, hung, and gibbeted in the chains he so much dreaded.'

We know that gibbet irons were measured and made at varying points in the proceedings and while most criminals post-Murder Act would have been measured for theirs before execution, prior to this it was often done after execution. Sometimes the irons were made in the intervening time between the sentence being passed and execution, which could be a matter of weeks but was usually days, and sometimes they were speedily made following execution to be available as quickly as possible.

There are a few cases of the prisoner being a blacksmith themselves and, as in the case of Sion y Gof, had to actually construct their own gibbet irons. Although this is the only case we know of for certain, there wouldn't have been more then one blacksmith in small communities so it may have happened at other times too. Although there is no mention of this in the case of Joseph Mutloe, he too was a blacksmith and even if he didn't make his own irons, he would have felt a strange affinity with the chains, as it could so easily have been his undertaking, rather than him being the one to wear them. Blacksmithing had been his livelihood, and the amount of time he spent working closely with iron would have given the prospect of the gibbet chains an odd intimacy to the whole proceedings. From the Gloucester Journals:

1742
Dec 7. Gloucester, Dec 4. Last Wednesday, between Two and Five in the Afternoon, JANE CLARKE, Widow of JASPER CLARKE, of Rodborough in this County, was

barbarously murdered (as suppos'd) by a Man that was seen at her House about Two the same Afternoon. – NB. He is tall, thin, very ill looking Fellow, near six Foot high, with small Bow legs; and had on, when seen at the said House, a light colour'd ragged Coat with White Metal Buttons and flash'd Sleeves, a red and white spotted Handkerchief, and a dirty Cap. The Murder was committed as follows: She was strangled with a Handkerchief, and her Skull fractur'd with a Wool Card, that lay by her with the End of it bloody; after which, the Villain took off the Fingers two Gold Rings; and one Gold Signet, the Posies as yet unknown; and then rifled the House, and left his own bloody Coat and Waistcoat with small Mohair Buttons, and a narrow old Hat unloop'd: By his Discourse he appears to be a Herefordshire Man, and by Trade a Blacksmith; and 'tis thought he was seen at Nailsworth Yesterday Morning, in the same brown Coat and Hat, with a Handkerchief full of Linnen.

1743

Bath, Dec 14. Yesterday JOSEPH MUTTLO, of Herefordshire, a Blacksmith, was apprehended here, on Suspicion of murdering JANE CLARKE, Widow, of Rodborough in Gloucestershire; and some of the Things that were lost out of the Deceased'd House were found upon him; (of which Murder and Robbery a particular Account was given in our Journal of the 7th Instant). He acknowledged the Fact, and that he sold the Rings in High Street, Bristol, one of them for 12 s. And the other two for 10 s. 6 d. The Reason for murdering her, he says, was because she would not give him some Money he ask'd her for: He is committed to the County Gaol of Somerset.

Gloucester, Feb 19. This Day was brought to our Castle, by Habeas Corpus, from Shepton Mallet Bridewell in Somersetshire, JOSEPH MUTTLOE, charg'd with the Murder of JANE CLARKE of Rodborough in this County.

Gloucester, Mar 12. Last Wednesday the Assizes ended here, when the six following Persons received Sentence of Death, viz. JOSEPH MUTLOE, for the barbarous Murder of JANE CLARKE, Widow, of Rodborough. The Prisoner had little to say in his Defence, only that he wanted her to give him some Money, which she refus'd to do, and in a Passion threw a Wool Card at him, which he threw at her again, and kill'd her; and then he rifled the House, and took off some Rings from her Fingers, which he sold at Bristol.

JOSEPH MUTLOE is order'd to be executed on Rodborough Hill, on Tuesday the 22d instant.

Gloucester, Mar 26. Last Tuesday JOSEPH MUTLOE was executed on Rodborough Hill, and afterwards hung in Chains, for the Murder of JANE CLARKE, of that Parish, Widow. He confessed the Fact, and desired the Spectators to pray for him.

The original description of Joseph Mutloe before he was caught outlines a man who was 'very ill looking', perhaps a further sign of how desperate some of these men were before they felt driven to rob and murder for money.

The location of gibbets could be a tricky business. The reasoning behind placing them at the scene of the crime may be sound, but it also seems quiet macabre, almost like a memorial. When John Codlin took a ride home with Simon Pottill in Norfolk in 1743, it was as the pair approached Pottill's house that Codlin attacked him and slit his throat. He then took Pottill's purse and, cutting the horse free from the carriage, rode it back to Norwich. When Codlin was caught and sentenced to execution then hanging in chains, there was no doubt about where his gibbet would be placed. The murder had been committed close to Pottill's house at Bunwell and that was where his murderer was left hanging on the gibbet.

There are no reports to say whether Pottill's family were living in the house, but it can't have been easy for anyone who knew him to see this spectacle hanging right outside his home. Although most gibbets were erected as close to the scene of the crime as possible, this was sometimes thought to be improper and sometimes families of victims or the hanged men asked for the gibbets to be moved due to the distress it caused them. Once a gibbet had been erected and the man hanged there in chains, it can't have been a simple undertaking to move the whole structure and this was only done on rare occasions where it was felt to be justified. The description of William Jobling's gibbet post being sunk into the slake in a 1½ ton stone base, shows the expected permanency of these constructions. To dig this back out and transport the whole structure to another location, then sink it into the ground once more, must have been an arduous task, but sometimes deemed necessary.

The Rev. Thomas Hunter committed a cruel and vengeful murder on two children near Edinburgh in 1770. Hunter had been having an affair with the maid who attended the house of the two little boys to whom he was teacher. One day the children witnessed Hunter and this girl in a compromising situation and they immediately told their parents. Although the maid was dismissed, Hunter was kept on as teacher to the boys, a mistake Mr and Mrs Gordon, the boys' parents, would come to regret. Hunter soon found his chance to take his revenge on the two boys for separating him from his lover. He first explained to the boys why they had to die, for giving away his secret, and then he slit their throats. The murder had been witnessed by a passer-by and there was no doubt as to Hunter's guilt. He confessed the fact without any remorse and was sentenced to death. Such was the horror of this crime, Hunter was chained to the floor in his prison cell. And the demand for his blood was so high, there had to be a very bloody punishment. Before his execution, Hunter's hands were cut off, he was hanged till he was dead and then hung in chains between Edinburgh and Leith, the knife with which he committed the murders being stuck through his hands, and his hands then fixed above his head at the top of the gibbet in a grisly and macabre display of his body parts.

If this gruesome display was meant to bring any comfort to the two boys' parents, it certainly didn't. The daily sight of Hunter's corpse hanging in his gibbet irons proved too much for the Gordons to bear. Mr Gordon petitioned the sheriff to have the gibbet moved to a more distant site, as it was causing his grief at losing his boys to be evermore intense. Rather than the constant sight of justice being done helping the parents, it was simply intensifying their grief and prolonging their anguish. The sheriff agreed to the request and the gibbet was moved to the small village of Broughton.

The Case of Jacob Saunders

Jacob Saunders of Reading was a lifelong criminal who murdered farmer Blagrave in 1723 for money. He beat Blagrave viciously and on discovering the man had very little money on his person, beat him some more in frustration. Blagrave died some days later, but never identified Saunders for the crime. It was by a witness who had seen the pair drinking together that evening and Saunders's bad character, plus his wife's testimony, that brought Saunders to trial and sentencing. It seems everyone knew what a bad apple Saunders was. He confessed and was due to be executed and hung in chains at the scene of the crime, but villagers succeeded in having the location changed, perhaps on account of a more suitable location already existing nearby, Gallows Tree Common. Still, this is unusual and no such sensibilities to the preferences of the inhabitants living close to gibbets were normally considered before they were erected. From the Newgate Calendar:

> He was sentenced to be hanged in chains at the spot where the shocking deed was perpetrated. However, as this place was near the village of Caversham, the inhabitants prevailed to have it done on a heath about four miles higher in Oxfordshire, called Gallows-Tree Common, from a tree in it, one arm of which grows into another tree, and forms the likeness of a gallows. Here a gibbet was erected. On Monday, about the middle of March, 1723, the wretch was brought to his execution. He was turned off without any pity, and immediately after he was dead he was hung up in irons.

It seems likely from the report that there was an outcry of sorts from the inhabitants of Caversham who did not want this proposed monstrosity in their community. As there is a suggestion at times that gibbeting was performed, at least in part, to appease the community where murders had occurred and to give them a sense of justice being done, in this case too the people of the community had to be appeased.

And then there was Joseph Armstrong. Armstrong was footman to Captain William Pierce A'Court and his wife Katherine in 1776 in Cheltenham. Katherine had Armstrong's card marked as soon as she met him and when items started to go missing, she told her husband to fire him. Armstrong was to be gone, but not before he slipped arsenic into Katherine's tea. Armstrong was soon caught and sentenced to death by hanging and afterwards to be sent to the surgeons for dissecting. Armstrong, just prior to his execution, asked for some time alone in his cell to contemplate, but when the gaolers went back in he was found hanged by his own leather strap. It seems the reason for hanging himself in private like this was to spare himself the indignity of the public spectacle of hanging before a crowd. But there was a crowd and they wanted their spectacle. So, the order for dissection was changed and Armstrong was hung in chains. The crowd got their day's entertainment and more, and Armstrong got the one punishment he had so tried to avoid.

Chapter 3

Infamy

From the Murder Act 1752:

> WHEREAS horrid crime of murder has of late been more frequently perpetrated than formerly, and particularly in and near the metropolis of this kingdom, contrary to the known humanity and natural genius of the British nation: and whereas it is thereby become necessary, that some further terror and peculiar mark of infamy be added to the punishment of death, now by law inflicted on such as shall be guilty of the said heinous offence.

It's unlikely anyone at the time of the Murder Act being passed had any idea just how infamous being hung in chains would make these criminals. Infamy is a curious thing. It is all at once self-defeating. The people who have committed heinous offences, the likes of which make us shudder, are remembered, celebrated, and even forgiven, while their victims go forgotten. Although these murderers and violent robbers may have been treated severely at the time, time shifts the lay of the land and as years pass we view these men with more sympathy. We are intrigued by their lives and the events that ran up to the terrible offence, we are endlessly fascinated by what it takes to step beyond the line we ourselves won't cross. And these men pass into legend and become not infamous, but with the growing sympathy towards them and a degree of forgiveness for what they did, famous.

The notoriety of murderers and the terrible things they do has been long in our psyche. Today we write books about murderers, make documentaries and fictionalised movies, we examine the details of what drives people to do such terrible things, and murderers become household names. We, as a society, want to know what these monsters have done and why they did it. We immortalise murderers. It's an uncomfortable thought, but we remain today fascinated by this most horrific crime, and we always have been.

But we are also interested in completing the story of a murderer by seeing them punished. We don't want our murderers to have a happy ending, we don't want them rehabilitated and back in our society. We want to see them punished and punished hard. Part of this is down to our own detachment from what these people are and the things they do. It's impossible for the majority of us to imagine committing such terrible acts, and so it intrigues us, but it also creates in us the belief that these people are so unlike us they are separate from 'normal' people, and should be treated as such, even after they have died.

In the time of gibbeting there may not have been books and films created about the lives of murderers, but we were still fascinated enough to want to remember them. We did this in various ways. Newspaper articles pored over the details of the crimes and reinforced our belief that these people were monsters, depraved and wicked, evil. And the locations of murders, and especially gibbets, have been cemented in our history by the naming of roads, lanes, hills, walks, and even songs. The punishment of hanging in chains was rare and that perhaps goes some way to explaining why we couldn't let go of the image of it. Today we can walk along a street that bears the name of a man who was gibbeted there. We don't know it, but these lanes and hills weave through our landscape with the ghosts of terrible crimes and equally terrible punishments still trapped within them. We can even visit areas in our landscape that bear memorials and plaques to keep the memory alive of what happened there. Some of these memories of gibbeting are laid bare, and some are tucked under nothing but a name.

Robin Down's Lane

In 1767 Robin Down (or Robert Downe) walked along this road playing his flute as he always did. Robin had learning difficulties and was well known as a 'half-wit' in Mansfield, Nottinghamshire, at the time. He was prone to fits of temper, but he was thought to be harmless and most people in the village helped him out and gave him food. One day, however, as he walked along the lane, a group of boys began following him, taunting him. Thomas Greenwood was a deaf mute and it's unlikely he really knew what he was involving himself in, but the other boys encouraged him to be loud in his actions and to make fun of Robin by gesturing at him. Robin's temper snapped and he pulled a knife on the boy.

This sad story doesn't get any better, as Thomas died of his wounds and Robin was arrested for his murder. The story goes that the jury at Robin's trial were aware of his learning problems and wanted to acquit him on these grounds, but the judge didn't agree and devised a test for measuring Robin's intelligence. He offered Robin one small gold coin and one large worthless coin. His reasoning was that if Robin chose the gold coin and not the bigger one he was intelligent enough to also understand what he was doing when he murdered Thomas. Robin chose the gold coin and his fate was sealed. Robin was publicly executed on Gallow's Hill just outside Nottingham, and then his gibbet erected at the scene of the crime in Mansfield. The road that Robin had walked along that day where this terrible twist of fate had occurred, is still called Robin Down's Lane today.

Walford's Gibbet

John Walford of Over Stowey in Somerset was said to be good looking, hard working, and pleasant, though writer Thomas Poole, who knew John, did note that he possessed 'strong passions'. It was these passions that ultimately proved to be John's undoing. John Walford and Anne Rice were engaged to be married in 1787 when John met Jane Shorney. History has been unkind to Jane and describes her as 'disgustingly dirty, slovenly of dress, squat, stupid creature'. People loved John, so Jane got the blame for what happened. While it's true that Jane did become pregnant with John's child at this time, John can hardly have been blameless. He never denied that Jane's child was his and he agreed to marry her. John would later say that Jane taunted him about his love for Anne and three weeks after their wedding he finally snapped.

When John confessed to Jane's murder he said the devil had him. Whether it was the devil, or his 'strong passion', his flaring temper and his frustration at the situation he was in, a situation of his own making, he grabbed her by the throat and beat her with a hedge post until her skull was fractured. Not content with that, he slit her throat and dumped her body in a ditch, now known as Dead Woman's Ditch. John Walford was arrested and sentenced to death by hanging. Anne was present and spoke to John before he was executed, apparently still showing love and sympathy for the man who had slept with someone else while they were engaged, and then brutally murdered her when he couldn't escape the consequences of what he had done. But consequence had caught up with him and he was hanged until dead. His body was then hung in chains on a nearby hill. Today there is a post by a bend in the road that marks the spot, bearing the words 'Walford's Gibbet'.

Winter's Gibbet

In 1791 William Winter had returned from transportation for his previous crimes of burglary and stealing an ass. He went back to his native Northumberland and promptly set about continuing his criminal lifestyle. With the assistance of two women who had already marked old Margaret Crozier as a woman of means, Winter murdered and robbed Crozier in the village of Raw. Winter was arrested and hanged at Newcastle, then his body brought back to the Northumberland moors and a gibbet erected at Elsdon. The two women accomplices were also executed and their bodies sent for dissection. It's said the original gibbet post was cut down and used for local cures, but a replica now stands in its place. At the foot of the imposing post is a large stone with a plaque embedded into it, detailing the crime and the punishment, it bears the words 'Winter's Gibbet'.

Tom Otter's Lane

We know quite a lot about Tom Otter, he made sure of that. Tom Otter was a 28-year-old man from Nottinghamshire. At 5 ft 9 in tall, he was said to be stout but handsome, and we can only guess that he was both handsome and charming, as he managed to marry twice without divorcing, and see both women pregnant in a very short space of time. Tom Otter was a bigamist, and much worse. He first married Martha Rawlinson at Eakring, Nottinghamshire on 22 November 1804. It was a shotgun wedding and their daughter was born a month after their nuptials. We can only assume that while Tom liked the thrill of the chase he wasn't so keen on following this through into family life and responsibilities. He swiftly left his wife and daughter behind in search of work and travelled into Lincolnshire.

Fair enough, you might think, he needed work, but as soon as Tom Otter crossed the county border he became Tom Temporal and began passing himself off as a widower using his mother's maiden name. He didn't intend going back to his family at this point and he quickly married 24-year-old Mary Kirkam, also by this time pregnant by Otter, in a second shotgun wedding. Mary was eight months pregnant at the time of this wedding, so a pattern was beginning to emerge. Sadly for Mary, Tom Otter was feeling the pressure of two wives and two children. The couple travelled from their wedding ceremony to The Sun Inn at Saxilby. They left the inn after a meal and drinks and on the road between Saxilby and Darnsey Nook, Tom Otter (or Temporal) savagely murdered his new wife and unborn child.

It was mere hours after their wedding and Tom beat Mary's head almost from her body with a wooden club, then tossed her body into a ditch. Mary's body was discovered the next morning and she was buried in Saxilby. Whatever Tom Otter's state of mind had been at the time, he wasn't very careful or discreet. A witness reported having seen him walking around carrying a wooden club earlier on the day of the murder and he was soon arrested for the killing of his new bride. His trial lasted five hours and his sentence was first to be executed and then dissected, as was the norm at the time. However, the horror of what he had done and the full story of who he was prompted the judge to alter this first sentence and Tom's body was ordered to be hung in chains following his execution in 1806. It's said Otter showed no shame or remorse about what he had done, but went to the gallows with a bowed head and resignation.

The remains of Tom Otter stayed in the gibbet where it hung until 1850. In this time the site became popular with gypsies who knew they could camp there in peace as no one else ever ventured up to the gibbet. One of the gypsies who camped there, Ashena Brown, told tales about the gibbet when she was an old woman – and the story of how and where her brother was born is especially surprising. Ashena Brown said that when her mother went into labour she sat at the foot of Tom Otter's gibbet to give birth. It was a windy night, the tents were blowing around in the gale, and the gibbet offered the woman some shelter. It was here that her baby boy was born, with the gibbet banging around in the wind above them. So, when it came to naming this new baby boy, Tom seemed like the only choice. This gypsy boy grew up to be known as Tom o'the gibbet. It's said that the wooden club used by Tom Otter to murder Mary was kept for many years following, and that on the night of the murder every year it would go missing from wherever it was kept and would appear again the next day covered in blood. This is a fun and ghostly tale, and the gypsy boy named after the gibbeted man beneath whose remains he was born is fascinating, but there is an even more lasting way in which we remember Tom Otter. Off the Gainsborough Road, near Drinsey Nook in Lincolnshire, runs Tom Otter's Lane and you can drive along it today.

Haslett's Pond

We know that Robert Haslett's body was still hanging in its gibbet six years after it had been placed there in 1770, thanks to the writings of a passer-by, but in fact it was there a lot longer than that. In 1809 the Enclosure Act marked the privatisation of common land and it was then that one Michael Hall bought the land on which Haslett's gibbet stood, and the gibbet was still there. Michael Hall had plans for this land that didn't include such a horrific spectacle and he removed the gibbet. But up until this point, and following Haslett's execution, this area of land in Gateshead was a bleak place that spoke of crime and grisly consequences, and no one would have travelled by, or walked here, without feeling the icy chill of Haslett's ghost lurking around. The Reverend James Murray, certainly a sympathiser of Haslett's, wrote that the gibbet stood by a small body of water which reflected Haslett's shadow. He suggested that this small lake would draw tourists because of its ghostly connotations juxtaposed with its beauty. This small body of water was from this point named Haslett's pond. It's visibly marked as such on the 1887 Ordnance Survey map of Gateshead, though following this there is no further mention of it. Sadly, when Michael Hall bought this land he filled the lake in to make way for his plans for redevelopment. Haslett's pond might not be there today, but for over a hundred years this landmark did bear the name of the gibbeted man.

Broughton Lane

In February 1791 Spence Broughton and John Oxley travelled from London to Sheffield to rob the Sheffield to Rotherham mail. It's said there was only a French bank note on board and the pair didn't profit much, but they did appear to get away with it … for a while. In October Oxley was arrested for a separate robbery in Cambridge and admitted to his part in the previous robbery, citing Broughton too. Broughton was soon apprehended and arrested. After snitching on Broughton, his partner in crime, Oxley managed to escape, leaving Spence Broughton to take the rap. Broughton was found guilty of robbing the mail, was sentenced to death and that his body should be hung in chains. Broughton's body was gibbeted on Attercliffe Common close to the scene of the crime. It seems the criminal had become famous already as it's reported that 40,000 spectators arrived on the first day to view Broughton's body; the landlord of the nearby inn, The Arrow, said the passing trade made him a fortune. Broughton's body remained in its gibbet until 1827 when the land was bought by Henry Sorby who removed it, not because he didn't want this exhibit on his land, but because he was tired of trespassers trampling over his land to see it. By this time the public was becoming more sympathetic to the criminals whose bodies were left hanging for years as a spectacle, and many were questioning the barbaric practice. The fame Spence had attracted seems to have marked him out for particular sympathy. The *Sheffield Register* in 1792 says,

> the behaviour of these unhappy men was singularly devout
> and penitent – and of Broughton in particular, was marked
> with a degree of fortitude and resignation, seldom observed
> in persons in his unfortunate circumstance.

In 1867 excavations of cellars were underway for new housing on Clifton Street, Attercliffe Common. A large oak post and framework were discovered and it was soon confirmed that this was the gibbet of Spence Broughton. The frame and post were taken to the Red Lion Inn near to the site and left in the garden for visitors to see it. As with his original gibbeting, large crowds flocked to the site to see this remnant of the punishment he received. It's said his gibbet irons were made into toasting forks and part of his bones incorporated in a bowl! Broughton was famous, and most likely because gibbeting was such a rare occurrence everybody knew about this case. Songs and poems were written about him, such as *Spence Broughton's Lament* by Joseph Mather:

> Hark, his blood, in strains so piercing,
> Cries for justice night and day;
> In these words which I'm rehersing,
> Now methinks I hear him say—
> 'Thou, who art my spirit's portion
> In the realms of endless bliss,
> When at first thou gav'st me motion
> Knew that I should come to this'

Broughton's infamy doesn't stop there. A pub stands close to the place of the gibbeting today, named The Noose and Gibbet, with a mock-up gibbet and body hanging from a post outside the pub. The pub is situated on Broughton Lane, Attercliffe. This gambling addict who made the life-changing decision of robbing the mail now has a road named after him. And what of his accomplice, John Oxley, who disappeared and got off scot-free? In 1793 Sheffield newspapers reported that John Oxley had been found in a barn on Loxley Moor, Sheffield, dead from cold and hunger. Ironically the same moor Francis Fearne had been gibbeted on in 1782. Francis Fearne's gibbet is said to have fallen down in the bad weather of 1797, so the skeleton of Sheffield's famous murderer would have been hanging in its chains when John Oxley took refuge there. John Oxley may not have faced the gibbet, but he did die of cold and starvation right next to one. Spence Broughton's last letter to his wife from prison and the subpoena for his trial attendance are held in store by Sheffield Museums. Although he was certainly guilty of his offence, to most people the punishment seems to have been too much, and although visitors loved to gawk at his body and the remnants of the punishment for years after, in hindsight he is viewed with sympathy and even some charm.

Old Parr Road

Some cases of gibbeted murderers and robbers are lost to history and all that remains is folklore and a road named after the defendant. Such is the case with Old Parr Road in Banbury. We do know that in 1746 a convicted murderer was executed and his gibbet hung in this location. His name was Parr. Perhaps, as with other cases, he was remembered because gibbeting was so rare in this area, or perhaps because of the nature of his crime, but we'll never know. All that remains is the Old Parr Road, a lasting legacy of a gibbeted murderer.

Ralph's Lane

Ralph Smith was no petty criminal or opportunist. The crime he committed in 1792 was not his first and it wasn't driven by desperation or terrible circumstances. Ralph Smith was a hardened criminal. He had recently returned from Australia where he had been transported for an earlier crime, when he arrived in Frampton, Lincolnshire. Ralph Smith broke into the cottage of 70-year-old Gentle Sutton and murdered him, then stole a claret-coloured coat and waistcoat, two pairs of white buckskin breeches, a scarlet waistcoat, one new bottle-green coat, a striped velvet waistcoat and five silver teaspoons. Smith stood little chance of getting away with it. He was known to be a criminal recently returned from transportation overseas and when a young eyewitness gave a full description and said he had seen Smith at the cottage that day, Ralph was arrested in Fiskertin where he was attempting to sell the clothing. He was executed on 16 May at Lincoln Castle and his body was then taken back to the scene of the crime to be hung in chains. Ralph Smith was the last person to be gibbeted in the area of Boston, Lincolnshire, and perhaps for that reason, or perhaps because he was such a famous criminal, his name went down in history. Not only is the road where this happened called Ralph's Lane, but there is also a plaque at the roadside which marks the spot of the gibbet. It's said that the gibbet post, made of an old oak tree, was cut up and used by locals for various things, one being a tobacco bowl which is now on display in the Guildhall Museum. Part of the oak post was used for a gatepost by a farmer in Spitfield Lane, just off Ralph's Lane.

Curry's Point

Just north of Whitley Bay a wild and rugged headland looks out to the north sea. This beautiful spot in the north east of England, which faces the white pillar of St Mary's lighthouse, was once the site of a murder and the post-mortem punishment for it. In 1739 Michael Curry was arrested for the murder of Robert Shevill, the landlord of the Three Horseshoes Inn at Hartley. Curry was a glass worker from Seaton Sluice and the rumour was that Shevill's wife urged Curry to murder her husband so that the two could be together and profit. Curry tried to wriggle free of the crime when he was arrested by stating he was with sailors and smugglers on the quayside in South Shields at the time of the attack. However, this didn't wash and he was sentenced to execution and hanging in chains for cutting Robert Shevill's throat with a razor. Curry was executed in Newcastle and transported back to this spot to be hung on the gibbet in sight of the scene of the crime. It's said he met his death with resignation and had no words to speak, but he did write a confession in which he owned up to the murder but stated that Shevill's wife had no part in it. As Curry hung in his gibbet, rumours gathered that someone was planning to cut him down and bury him. A warning was issued in the press that this was forbidden and Curry must hang between heaven and earth and not be afforded a burial.

Today a plaque is laid in a standing stone on the spot where the gibbet once stood and explains the story to visitors, and why this piece of land is named 'Curry's Point'.

Kenneth's Mount

A small hill in Aberdeenshire where Kenneth Leal robbed the mail of £270 and was hung in chains at the site following his execution, is called Kenneth's Mount. His remains, still in their gibbet irons, were also discovered years later at this site. Though most of the irons and remains were reburied, parts of the head piece were carried off as 'trophies'; grim souvenirs.

Tom Lee's Smidy

In 1766 Tom Lee murdered Dr Richard Petty for money. The pair had been to a cock fight at Kettlewell and were walking back to Grassington in Yorkshire. Petty must have thought his luck was in when he won a substantial amount of money at the cock fight that evening, but it was his bad luck to be in the company of the blacksmith Tom Lee. By all accounts Tom Lee was a hard man. He liked to gamble, he liked to drink, and he was known for his temper. After stopping at an inn or two on the way home, Tom Lee murdered Richard Petty and took his winnings. After an unsuccessful attempt at hiding the body, Tom was soon arrested for the murder, but he was acquitted at the trial due to lack of evidence. Tom Lee went back to his life in Grassington and must have been quite smug in getting away with this cruel murder. However, two years later what Tom Lee had done caught up with him. Someone whose conscience caused them problems came forward with evidence that it was indeed Tom Lee who had committed this murder. Lee was sentenced to death this time and was hung at Tyburn in July 1768 and his body then hung in chains on what is now known as Gibbet Hill, Grass Woods. It's said that souvenir hunters were quickly at the gibbet and the silver buckles from his shoes were the first items to go. Reports say that even parts of his bones were stolen. Today a plaque adorns the wall of what was once Tom Lee's 'smidy'. Although it does state that this was the blacksmith's shop owned by the 'notorious' Tom Lee, it doesn't give us any further details about his crimes or punishment. He is still remembered in the village and beyond and his ghost is said to haunt Grass Woods.

Toby's Walks

In the village of Blythburgh, just past Southworld in Suffolk there walks the memory of one of the most unsettling cases of gibbeting in history. In 1750 Tobias Gill, or Black Toby as he was known, was a drummer in Sir Robert Rich's Regiment of Dragoons. It's often been suggested that he was named 'black toby' because of his lewd and unruly behaviour, but there seems little doubt, owing to songs of the time and the fact that we know black people were employed as musicians in the regiments, that his name was given to him because of the colour of his skin. Toby did like to drink though, there's no doubt of that, but getting drunk wasn't a crime. Rich's regiment were positioned at Suffolk on account of the troubling rise in smuggling and though many soldiers had a lot of sympathy with smugglers and certainly benefited from their loot, the regiment can't have been popular with these lawless sea thieves. They probably weren't popular with many people at all. It was noted in the *Derby Mercury* at the time that Toby Gill had gained a reputation for drinking and causing trouble and was banned from many inns and ale houses. We need to take this with due scepticism, as he wouldn't have been the only one to be turned away from inns, but we also need to consider the question of his colour playing a part in his being singled out.

One night when the men had a little too much to drink, as they often did, it's said that Toby wandered onto the common in the dark. With only moonlight for guidance and uneven under foot, Toby came across Anne Blackmore, a young servant girl. What Anne was doing out there on the common at night we don't know, but when she was found dead the next morning only Toby's name came up in connection to the death. He was arrested for murder, even though it was stated that there was not a mark on Anne's body and no sign of force or a struggle. Some reports say Toby was found laying drunk and asleep next to her lifeless body and it was this that caused the presumption of his guilt, while others say it was simply the fact that he wandered off in the night that made others point the finger. Either way, Toby was convicted of murder, with the rumour that he had also raped the girl, and he was sentenced to death by hanging. Although many reports, including one from the *Ipswich Journal*, say that Toby was gibbeted alive on the very spot where Anne's body was found, this is almost certainly not true. Toby Gill was hanged by the neck until he died and then taken to the gibbet cage which was hung as close to the scene of the crime as possible, but also in plain sight of the road used as the main route for the London mail. Toby had protested his innocence all along and continued to do so right up until his execution. Whether his colour swayed his fate or not, there is a lot of doubt about the murder ever happening. It seems to have been a simple case of poor Toby being in the wrong place at the wrong time; there was no evidence that Anne had been murdered at all (it's thought she most likely died of natural causes), and no evidence that Toby had anything to do with her death. Although the gibbet post used to hang Toby in chains remained on the spot for years after, all that is left to remind us now is an area of the common named Toby's Walks. It's said that Toby haunts this place and can be seen walking around in a drunken stupor with no grave and nowhere to go. Black Toby was also immortalised in this old Suffolk poem, which suggests it was thought at the time that he had strangled Anne with a handkerchief, although there was no mention in the trial of this and there wasn't any evidence of strangulation at all.

BLACK TOBY
(in dialect)
Fine momin sah, wot's thaat yaou ax
Wot plaace be thaat ahid ?
Woy thaat be Blybrer straate, tha's ware
I live, an' allers did;

An' yon's the chuch, but haps yaou know't
For these hare larst few yares
A mort o' fooks come round these paarts,
An' at the chuches stares;

For sure 'tis mighty 'musin' tew,
Ter hare the waay they torks;
Yus, hinder be the Wukhus, an'
These hare be Toby's Walks;

Hew's Toby? did I hare yaou saay?
Woy then, 'tis plain ter see
Yaou doan't belong ter these hare paarts,
Ware mought yar buthplaace be?

In Lunnon town! woy then in coorse
Yaou cou'nt be 'sposed ter know,
I'l tell yer wot I've allers heerd;
Yaou'll 'souse my bein' slow,

'Cos I haain't larnt ter spaake up shaarp,
Nor niver bin ter skule.
An' wen I sees fooks read an' write
I faals a blarmed owd fule;

But this hare's wot my grammother
Hev orfen towd ter me,

Infamy

An' she wore right a tough un, foor
She lived ter ninety three;

How more'n a hunderd yare agoo,
Wen good owd Goorge wore King,
An' England fowt the Frenchmin, as
I've heerd owd sowdjers sing;

A regiment o'sowdjers come
Along o'this hare rood,
An' laay in Blybrer Straate a waak,
A' lodgin' ware they could;

An' they'd a band o' music got,
With drummers tew oor three,
An' one o' these hare drummers chaps
Wore blaack as blaack could be;

Blaack Toby wore his Chrissen uaame,
His naature, 'twore thaat baadd
As iy'ry one as knowed 'm said
The devil wore his daad;

One ev'nin he wore stroamin' round
Good tidy full o'booze.
Wen a gal come gald'rin' down yon rood,
An arter har he goos;

Now wot he said oor done ter har
I caan't ezackly tell,
Foor yaou be bound 'twam't nuthin good.
An' baad tork doan't sound well;

Howsever she won't none o'him,
An' towd 'm so I spec
For arter har he went right quick
An' catcht har by the neck.

Har hankercher he then pulled out,
Which round har throot he tied,
An' then he hulled har on the ground.
An' graained har till she died;

An' then, 'tis wonndy straange to saay,
The drink began ter tell,
An' in drunkin kind o'slaape
Right by the coorpse he fell.

The next d' morn some laabrin' fooks
A comin from the Straate,
They see owd Toby i' the holl,
With the gal agin his faate;

An' as 'twere clear he kilt the gal,
Altho' he fowt 'm haard,
They took 'm up right out 'n hand,
An' kep 'm under guard;

The Crowner's Quest saat on the coorpse,
An' orl o' them agreed
As how 'twore plaain the gal wore kilt,
An' plaain hew done the deed;

They found as Toby done the job.
An' as he con'nt ha' bail;
They sent 'm orf ter Ipswich town,
An' hulled 'ni inter jaail.

An' there he laay till 'Sizes come.
An' senteneed 'm ter deth,
Sayin' as how he must be hung
On this hare wery heth;

They browt 'm tew the cross roods there,
An' hanged 'm up in chaains,
An' there he hung till he dropt down,
Wore out by winds and raains;

An' ef aat midnight time yaou stan'.
Jest ware them gallers stood,
Fooks saay yaoull hare a carriage come
A rattlin' down the rood.

Foure bosses blaack without no bids,
A Fun'ril bus behind,
A blaack maan settin' on the box
A drivin' loike the wind;

They saay 'cos Toby hain't no graave,
Noor yet no parsin' bell,
He're got ter come hare iv'ry night,
An' drive hisself ter hell.

The gals an' childen i' the plaace.
An' growed up wimmin tew,
They on't goo parst hare arter daark
Onless there be a crew;

But hinder come our Maaster's dorg,
So he bain't faar awaay,
He caan't abear us mardlin' so
I wish yaou Sab, Gooddaay.

Ernest R. Cooper

And The Notorious Eugene Aram

Eugene Aram was a very intelligent man. A teacher and intellect from King's Lynn, he discovered the link between the European languages and wrote great texts on the subject of the science of language. He could have been remembered for this, his great work, if it wasn't for a very dark period near the end of his life. It was while living in Knaresborough, Yorkshire, in 1744, a married teacher and respected member of the community, that things got weird. Aram became friends with shoemaker Daniel Clark. Clark was no ordinary shoemaker, he was married to a woman who had a fortune in trust, and which they were about to inherit.

71

Aram, meanwhile, had considerable debts. When Clark went missing there wasn't much alarm at first, but when Aram began paying off all his debts, fingers started to point and tongues began to wag. Aram clearly felt the pressure because suddenly, without warning, he upped and left his wife and family and started looking for teaching work elsewhere. In 1758 he was back in King's Lynn, his birthplace, teaching at the grammar school.

He might have thought at this point that he was safe, but when a skeleton was discovered back in Knaresborough, Aram was hunted down. It was Aram's wife, perhaps still bitter at the way her husband had deserted them, who named another man, Houseman, as Aram's accomplice in murder. Houseman admitted the fact, but in a twist to the story, stated that the skeleton was not Clark's because he knew where Clark's remains really were, because, yes, he had indeed helped Eugene Aram dispose of them. The second skeleton was found in a cave and Eugene Aram was convicted of murder. In 1759 he was executed and then hung in chains near the cave at Knaresborough. Perhaps because of who Eugene Aram was, his great intellectual brain and his high standing in the community, his story wasn't about to end there.

Aram's skull was of particular interest to surgeons and phrenologists, who wanted to find out what would make such an intelligent man do something so terrible. Phrenology was a popular new 'science' of the time that included identifying bumps on the skull to indicate different character traits and leanings. Certain areas of the brain were thought to be linked to certain behaviours and by 'feeling the bumps', phrenologists proposed they could predict a person's character and actions. Aram's skull was particularly important to phrenologists as he was both intelligent and a murderer. After surgeons and phrenologists had finished examining it, Aram's skull was passed to his remaining family members and after being passed down the line, it eventually made its way back to King's Lynn, where Aram's life had begun. The skull is now on display at the Stories of Lynn Museum, along with a skull fragment from Daniel Clark. The interest in this most unusual murderer has always been high and Aram has been immortalised in *The Dream of Eugene Aram*, a ballad by Thomas Hood, and *Eugene Aram* a novel by Edward Bulwer-Lytton, published in 1832. The novel was later adapted by W.G. Wills and staged as a play.

Chapter 4

Thieves and Pirates

Other than murder, there were three further offences for which you could be hung in chains in Britain – highway robbery, piracy, and robbing the mail. Robbing the mail and highway robbery are often lumped together, but robbing the mail was a particular crime all of its own and one which was viewed under a very dark hat. Highway robbery could be the holding up and robbing of individuals, and did sometimes involve murder, as did piracy. But all three of these crimes were punishable by death and hanging in chains, whether a murder had also been committed or not.

The highwayman, for fortune and fame!

> The wind was a torrent of darkness among the gusty trees,
> The moon was a ghostly galleon tossed upon cloudy seas,
> The road was a ribbon of moonlight over the purple moor,
> And the highwayman came riding—
> Riding—riding—
> The highwayman came riding, up to the old inn-door.

From *The Highwayman* by Alfred Noyes, 1906

The image of the highwayman has been romanticised and tinged with nostalgia over the years. The idea of a dapper man riding his horse along the highway, waiting for a carriage containing rich travellers who could, of course, easily afford to give their money to this enterprising opportunist, has been laid in our psyche like a brick in cement. But as with many fond ideas we hold of bygone eras, it wasn't quite like that if you lived at the time. These men who robbed on the highways may be thought of as having honour, and even as being gentlemanly about their robbing, but they were still thieves and they still held up coaches of terrified passengers or robbed anyone they happened to encounter walking along dim, barren roads at night. Perhaps it's something to do with the poetic sounding phrases 'stand and deliver', and 'your money or your life', and it certainly has something to do with our imagined vision of the way these men dressed and how mysterious they were.

Highwaymen have been given the treatment by writers of history and of fiction, but life for the highwayman himself, as well as his victims, was anything but romantic. The average life expectancy of a highwayman was 28. For most of the time these criminals were operating, there was no organised police force, so they could get away with their activities for quite some time. It was very difficult for constables to find and catch these thieves, but as their reputation spread, not many of them could keep up this criminal career for long. The penalty for highway robbery was death, and it was also one of the very few crimes aside from murder that carried the post-mortem punishment of gibbeting. With the highways at the time being such lawless and dangerous places, gibbeted highwaymen were placed on popular routes as a deterrent to other robbers. The site of these corpses swinging in the wind on the dark empty roads they once used as their hunting ground must have been as terrifying to travellers as encountering a highwayman alive. Many highwaymen saw their fellow criminals of the road executed and then hung in chains on the very same roads they frequented. But the lure of fortune, and fame, was too strong and most of them tipped their hat at the man hanging in chains, and kept to their criminal lifestyle.

Black Harry

The Peak District in Derbyshire was a particularly perilous place to travel in the eighteenth and nineteenth century. Stone markers were the only way of navigating your way around, and the wild sweeping moors made it easy to get lost, meaning travellers were easy pickings for highwaymen. Black Harry was the most famous highwayman who operated in Derbyshire, and is still famous today in this area. He preferred to rob the pack mule train that ran between Bakewell and Tideswell, something that may have softened the memory of him and given his legend an air of sympathy, but he did also target travellers on the turnpike road and it was this that put the fear into anyone facing such a journey.

The prospect of encountering Black Harry on the road was a terrifying one. His reputation, perhaps inflated and romanticised, went before him. But despite his fame and his success, eventually Black Harry was caught. As The Bow Street Runners became more prevalent and efficient in London, the idea swept across the country and it was an arm of this early organised police force in Castleton that captured the highwayman. Black Harry was hung at Derby gaol and then his body was placed in a gibbet on Wardlow Mires, easily visible to travellers on the road and also to any other would-be highwaymen. Today, you can walk on Black Harry Lane and visit Black Harry Gate near Stoney Middleton, remembering this famous highwayman and his gruesome end. The pathways, as they appear now, snake through the landscape and if you walk along these routes today it's still a mysterious place. Black Harry Lane winds around and it's impossible to see what's coming around the bend as you travel forward. It's eerily quiet and not many people use these routes now so it's easy to imagine how Black Harry could have hidden himself on these old roads and leapt out on unsuspecting travellers. Named after the man who terrorised the people in this area, something of him lingers in the air here and the lanes still feel thick with apprehension and a slight prickle of fear.

Jack Upperton

Jack Upperton could be thought of as an unfortunate and unlucky man. He was a poor labourer all his life, he owned no land and had no prospects; aged 60 he decided he'd had enough of living as a poor man and that it was time he took something for himself. Along with a friend and accomplice, Jack decided he could intercept the postman on the highway and find himself a small fortune. Together the pair waited for William Boldrey, the local postman, to travel along the highway between Lewes and Chicester. The two inexperienced highwaymen overpowered Boldrey and did rob of him of the money he had on him, however, Boldrey recognised Upperton and his fate was sealed. In 1771 Jack Upperton, poor labourer turned highwayman, was executed for his crime and his body placed in the gibbet on the road where the crime had been committed. It's said his body took two years to completely decompose and his gibbet was left standing long after. Jack may have been a thief, but this was his first offence and he never murdered anyone. This seems like rough justice to us today, as he received the same punishment as the most brutal and savage murderers in the country. And there is some evidence that the people in his community felt the same way. Upperton's descendants have long remembered the spot where the unlucky man was hung in chains and various markers and memorials have been placed there over the years. This seems to have been tolerated and allowed by the rest of the community as no one ever made any attempts to remove or prevent these dedications, perhaps leading us to the conclusion that Jack did have some sympathy among those who knew him. Today a post still stands in memory of Jack Upperton. Letters carved into a wooden plaque simply say 'J. U. 1771'.

Captain Jack (Jacques)

Captain Jack, as he was known, is a bit of a legend. On the wilds of Dartmoor his ghost roams, and at the Royal Anchor Inn in Liphook, Hampshire, they say his spirit still lingers after he was eventually cornered and shot in one of the bedrooms. There isn't much known about his life, except that he was a smuggler and highwayman and he was caught by excise men who weren't about to let him get away. If you go to the Royal Anchor and stay in bedroom six, you might just catch the memory of what happened there to this prolific robber, but he was actually executed and hung in chains on Gibbet Hill, Dartmoor.

Jerry Abershawe

The mystique we so love about the highwayman is often deepened by mysterious childhoods and hints of orphanage or difficult circumstances. That we can't solidify the facts of these men's early years only makes them more interesting to us. Jerry Abershawe's early life is steam in the cold air, it seems to take form sometimes, then it dissipates. But with no mention of him ever having a family, mother, father, or anyone close to him, it's safe to assume he was an orphan or unfortunate boy who quickly turned to a life of crime as a way to survive. Abershawe was just 17 when he began his criminal career, forming a gang that used an inn on the London Road between Kingston and Wimbledon as their base. This inn was the Bald Faced Stag, which in 1752 had been chosen as a better location for the gibbet of John Swan, the first man to be hung in chains following the Murder Act. Swan's gibbet had been placed close to this inn as it was the establishment he had collected his victim from and had been the victim's favourite pub. Although we don't know how long Swan's gibbet had stood at this location, even if it wasn't still there at this time, Abershawe and his accomplices in crime would have known about it. Abershawe was born in 1773, twenty-one years after John Swan's gibbet was erected, so this is something he is likely to have been aware of growing up. Was this why they chose this particular inn for their meetings to discuss their proposed crimes? Whether this gang was successful or not, Jerry soon went it alone and took up highway robbery. He must have realised that, travelling from London to Bath and other well-to-do areas of the south, some pretty wealthy people took the road through these parts and Jerry could make quite a living. But Jerry's sorry career, and life, were short lived. He was just 22 when two constables went searching for him with the express intention of arresting him. Jerry didn't think twice about shooting both of them and one of them died, adding to Jerry's list of terrible crimes. He was later arrested at an inn in Southwark and then convicted and sentenced to death. The Newgate Calendar reported on his execution:

> He was executed on Kennington Common, on the 3rd of August, 1795 in the presence of an immense multitude of spectators, among whom he recognised many acquaintances and confederates, to whom he bowed, nodded, and laughed with the most unfeeling indifference. He had a flower in his mouth, and his waistcoat and shin were unbuttoned, leaving his bosom open in the true style of vulgar gaiety; and talking to the mob, and venting curses on the officers, he died, as he had lived, a ruffian and a brute!

Jerry Abershawe was quite the character and most likely saw his own lifestyle of criminality as daring and exciting, and being a highwayman, flamboyant and charismatic. He died as he lived then, but following his execution his body was tarred and placed in a gibbet by the road where he had operated as a highwayman. At Tibbet's Corner today there is a wooden post with a decorative sign atop it, showing a dastardly highwayman. It's unlikely this post is an actual gibbet post, but it serves as a reminder of what happened here in far more dangerous travelling times. Jerry Abershawe is remembered for his sorry short life and his audacious crimes and lifestyle. By the London Road, where Jerry once wielded his gun at wealthy travellers, is Jerry's Hill.

John Brady

In 1800 John Brady, sometimes Burns, robbed Edward Burrell the mail boy on the highway. John took fifteen leather bags from Edward, the total cost within was 15 shillings, a considerable amount at the time. He was executed at Lancaster Castle and then hung in chains at Ashton where the robbery had taken place.

Patrick O'Brien

Patrick O'Brien came to England from Ireland looking for work when he was a young man. After a short time as a soldier he realised the pay in that profession wasn't nearly enough to support his drinking habit and he took to robbing on the highways. Patrick seems to have had little thought for the fate of others, he persuaded many young men to join him in his thieving lifestyle and often they hanged for the crime long before he did. But he did have friends, a fact that became clear when he was eventually caught for highway robbery and hanged at Gloucester in 1689. After hanging for what was deemed enough time he was cut down and his body given to his friends for burial. On the way to one of Patrick's friends' houses there were signs of life and to their surprise Patrick was indeed still breathing. His friends decided to tell no one about this and, gaining a promise from Patrick that he would alter his lifestyle and go straight, they all agreed to let him go on with his life as a new person. But highway robbery was now running in Patrick's blood and it wasn't long before he was back on the quiet night-time roads waiting for someone to hold up with his gun.

It was a year after his execution when he came upon a man on the highway who recognised him. It was the very same man Patrick had robbed before his execution. The same man whose robbery had, in fact, led to Patrick's execution. Patrick couldn't risk letting this man go and him spreading the word of Patrick's apparent resurrection so he took up his pistol and shot the man in the head. Up until this point, as far as we know, Patrick O'Brien had not been a murderer, but now he had opened the flood gates and went on a vicious rampage of burglary, rape, and multiple murders. At Lancelot Wilmot's house in Wiltshire, Patrick and four other men raped and murdered everyone inside, carried off all the valuables and then burned down the house. As Patrick was still 'dead' at this point, no one suspected him and he went about his villainous ways without fear of being caught. The game was finally up two years later when one of the four accomplices was arrested for another crime. This man confessed all his crimes and named Patrick in the deeds. Patrick was caught at Haymarket and this time there was to be no chance of mistake. Patrick was hanged until dead, but just to make sure he couldn't escape a second time, he was immediately hung in chains and left to rot on the gibbet.

Jocelin Harwood

Jocelin Harwood of Kent was known as a toe-rag from being a small boy. His father gave up on him when, aged 16, he stole money and belongings from his father and took off. From here Jocelin went to London and embarked on his criminal career. He wasn't particularly good at it and was caught for pickpocketing, spending three years in prison, before turning to the highways. Even here Jocelin faced some anxiety when not all his victims went quietly; his horse shot and he was wounded, which shocked him but also hardened him and gave him a new determination.

Along with two others he broke into the house of Sir Nehemiah Burroughs in Shropshire and set about plundering it. When Nehemiah's daughter suggested she would know him again after this time and would keep the secret, he realised that any one of the inhabitants of the house could name him, so he murdered them all. His two accomplices had not signed up for this and were so appalled by what Jocelin had done, they tied him up at the scene and left him there. Jocelin was caught the next day and sentenced to death by hanging. Jocelin Harwood was not a man to back down, no matter how shameful his situation, and he spat in the face of the judge at his trial. If the judge had been in any quandary about what sentence to pass this action would have sealed Jocelin's fate. He went to the gallows unrepentant and stated he would murder again if he could. After hanging till dead he was hung in chains for all to see what a pitiful man he was. He was just 23 when he died.

John Hawkins and James Simpson

When John Hawkins and James Simpson met a young man named Wilson, fate took hold of the three of them with a very firm grip. Hawkins and Simpson were already highwaymen and robbers, but Wilson was a gambling addict and found he needed some way of paying for this expensive lifestyle, and to pay off the debts he'd already built up. He quickly joined Hawkins and Simpson and set about highway robbery with them. Wilson had a conscience and this new criminal way of life didn't sit easily with him, but he did throw himself into this roguish behaviour for some time and with some enthusiasm. Along with Hawkins he robbed wilfully and the pair ran amok in a gallery and defaced some important pieces of art. The fun ended when they met back up with Simpson and went out on the highways together. When they stopped a carriage on the Hampstead Heath they got more than they bargained for. The gentlemen inside weren't about to give up easily and they immediately fired shots from within the carriage. One hit Hawkins on the shoulder. The gang weren't put off yet though and they carried on to Hyde Park where they tried to hold up another carriage. The driver didn't stop and when Wilson attempted to shoot the man he only wounded his own hand.

The debacle of this fateful night was too much for Wilson and he decided to put an end to it, even telling his mother he was in over his head and knew it had to stop before something serious happened to him. He told her he was sorry for what he'd done and his mother urged him to give himself up. But Hawkins and Simpson were planning to rob the Bristol mail, and had included Wilson in their plans. Whether he felt pressured to do this or whether he was willing, we don't know, but soon after the robbery had taken place Wilson was apprehended by the general postmaster. Wilson was pressured to give up his two accomplices and although he at first refused, when the postmaster revealed a letter he had and said it was written in the hand of one of the other two men, Wilson eagerly gave them up. It seems unlikely this letter really was written by Hawkins or Simpson, as it suggests the postmaster would not have needed Wilson's testimony if it was:

> SIR, — I am one of those persons who robbed the mail, which I am sorry for; and to make amends, I will secure my two companions as soon as may be. He whose hand this shall appear to be will, I hope, be entitled to the reward of his pardon.

But it certainly did the trick and Wilson gave them up without another thought. On 27 May 1722, John Hawkins and James Simpson were hanged at Tyburn and then hung in chains on Hounslow Heath. After a career as highwaymen, the pair were actually tried and sentenced for robbing the mail.

Tim Buckley

Tim Buckley was a vengeful man. He began his criminal career after being refused a loan of money from the landlord at whose pub he'd already drank away all his money. Later that same night, Tim broke into the inn and took the money he'd been refused, tying up and gagging the innkeeper and his family. The local constable was lenient and tried to force Buckley to a soldier's life instead of arresting him, but rather than seeing the mercy in this, Buckley raped the constable's wife and took the rings from her fingers. He robbed the pawnbroker who had sold on items pawned by Buckley, and stole money from the prosecutor who had previously sentenced him to burn in the hand for his crimes so far, meaning he was already branded with a letter to signify a previous crime. Tim Buckley never took responsibility for his actions and seemed to consider himself the victim and everyone else as offending against him.

This life couldn't go on and his criminal escapades eventually came to and end when he was 29 in 1701. Buckley was caught and convicted of robbing the prosecutor, but he escaped and promptly burned down the man's house. He'd gone too far this time and there was no turning back. From here things went from bad to worse for Buckley who rode onto the highway on his horse and ordered the next carriage along to stand and deliver. The gentlemen inside were not about to give up all they had; they got out of the carriage and challenged Buckley. In the fight that followed Buckley killed two of the men. This ended Tim's criminal career and his life. He was executed at Nottingham Gaol and hanged in chains on the road where he had committed murder.

There seems to be very little rhyme or reason to when the punishment of gibbeting was passed for highway robbery and when it was not. In most cases it was not. Sometimes the criminal appears to have been hung in chains as a further punishment because his career had been so prolific and he'd been getting away with it, sometimes it was because highway robbery turned into murder, and sometimes it seems to have been because the criminal had already been prosecuted for robbery, received a lesser sentence such as burning in the hand and then had, on release, gone straight back out on the highway. The judge may have felt the lesson was not being learned, or that he had nowhere left to go except to hang the robber and for further effect, and to show this wouldn't be tolerated, hanging in chains.

These were thieves, and they performed what might today be thought of as 'mugging'. They lay in wait on quiet roads at night and ordered anyone who travelled by to hand over their belongings. And yet we romanticised them. They had 'honour'. Perhaps at the time, when this was a common fright to face, we did not think of them with so much charm.

In letters to her sister, Jane Austen talks of her brother's concern that she might travel on a road known to be the favoured lair of highwaymen. He actively forbade it, such was the fear of this awful thing happening to his own sister.

Mail Robbers

Apart from highway robbery and piracy the other crime punishable by death and hanging in chains, other than murder, was robbing the mail. Robbing the mail was often caught up with highway robbery as one and the same, and as we see in the examples above, was often performed by criminals who did a little of both. The only difference being that this crime was perpetrated not against individuals, but the royal mail. It was usually carried out by experienced highwaymen, but sometimes it was an opportunist criminal or a first time criminal, like Jack Upperton. Robbing the mail seems to be the crime punishable by hanging in chains that the general public was most sympathetic towards, probably because it was aimed at an organisation and not an individual, much like a thief today stealing money from large corporations. In the newspapers and in general opinion following both the crime and the punishment, men who robbed the mail were excused and looked on as poor unfortunate souls.

Spence Broughton who robbed the Rotherham to Sheffield mail and was gibbeted at Atterclife, was exonerated in popular songs and ballads after his death. In a pamphlet now held in store at Sheffield Museums, titled 'The True and Illustrated Chronicles of the Last Man Gibbeted in Yorkshire, His Last Letter on the Eve of his Execution to his Wife and his Dying Confession in Verses Set to Music', Spence Broughton is painted as a man to be pitied, someone who was led astray by John Oxley and who took a far worse punishment than he deserved. He is often described as handsome and of good character.

This sympathising of mail robbers is seen in many cases. William Creak robbed the mail on Bagshot Heath, Surrey, in 1790. He was apprehended, tried, sentenced to death and to be hung in chains at the scene of the crime. Reports from the time talk of William being an unfortunate man, much lamented for his death, and that he was persuaded from his honest way of life by his wife's brother. It's said that his brother-in-law, Kitson, orchestrated the crime, took half of the loot, and then dobbed Creak in to the authorities. The Newgate Calendar talks of the struggle to come to terms with what happened and the 'detestation of such individual treachery'. The blame is put squarely at Kitson's feet and Creak is looked on with some nostalgia, even using his family situation as some sort of excuse for what he did:

> He had a large family, bore an excellent character among his neighbours, and his credit was still good with his merchants in London. Unsuspicious of others, he had given credit to a considerable amount, and was deceived in promises of payment. It also appeared that this was the only piece of iniquity, in which he had been concerned.

It's hard to find such sympathy and excuses made for any other crimes that resulted in gibbeting or even the death penalty.

Robbing the mail deserves a category all of its own. Set apart from highway robbery, or even just robbery. Robbing the mail at the time of capital punishment was one of the most serious offences a person could commit. Why? The mail is sent 'on his/her majesty's service'. This is official business and anyone who interferes with this is interfering with the king or queen's business. Disrupting the mail in any way is still an offence today, though punishment is a lot more lenient. In the seventeenth, eighteenth and nineteenth century, robbing the mail was something you only did if you were desperate, too arrogant to think you'd get caught, or you were a very tenacious and clever criminal indeed.

William Lewin

William led a large and full life. By the time of his arrest and conviction in 1791 he was a bigamist, a serial mail robber, and had many aliases. His criminal life led him to wander through various identities in various towns in Britain. He was born William Lounds in Congleton, Cheshire, in 1759. He married a local girl who was pregnant by him at the time, but he soon left this family in pursuit of a new life. In 1785 he married Amy Clarke of Alfreton, Derbyshire, they had two children, and in Amy William found his most perfect partner in crime. It seems Amy was quite happy to follow her husband in his criminal lifestyle and more than that, she actively helped him. William Lounds would become William Clarke, William Brown, William Hope, William Maul, William Hutchinson, and lastly on his arrest, William Lewin.

William robbed the mail all over the country, and enjoyed the fruits of his success. Perhaps once he realised he could do this and get away with it, it was very difficult to stop. But although his wife clearly loved and supported him, this way of life couldn't go on forever. He was caught in Exeter, after robbing the mail there, and was taken to Chester Castle where he was imprisoned. In prison William undertook a few daring and clever attempts at escape, sometimes helped by his wife who smuggled various implements into the gaol, including iron and clay to make impressions of keys and meld them, and laudanum to drug the guards. Although these attempts at escape were persistent and used great initiative, ultimately they were to no avail. William was executed for robbing the mail and his body hung in chains on the most elevated part of Helsby Tor, eight miles from Chester. William was a prolific mail robber, and it seems the authorities wanted everyone to know that they did not tolerate this. He was positioned so that he would be 'confpicuoufly seen, and, by means of glafes, is vifible to the whole county, moft parts of Lancaihire, Flintfhire, Denbighthire, Shropihire, Der byfhire.' As Albert Hartshorne tells us in his book *Hanging in Chains*, citing 'The Trial of William Lewin 1791'.

But William was repentant. He never killed anyone and there is no mention of any violence in any of his crimes of robbing the mail. It seems that, above all, he regretted being caught and the letters between him and his wife from prison show a tortured mind and an anxiousness to exonerate his wife of any involvement:

> DʙAk WIFʙ, God only knows with what anxiety of mind
> I have waited for an opportunity of fending thefe few lines
> to thee, my ruined and diftrefed wife, Ruined did I fay? yes,
> ruined; and by whom? By me, her wretched hufband. Oh!
> diftragting thought! And muft I never, never fee thee more?
> thou beft and moft faithful of thy fex. Oh! cruel, cruel men,
> that thus debar a poor wretch, like me, the only with I have
> on earth, debar me from the companion of my life, and of my
> woes beft foother. Oh had I but taken thy gentle admonitions
> and cordial advice, I had not, as I am, been doomed a wretch,
> like this, loaded with ignominious chains in this dreary prifon.
> But what are chains, or bolts, or prifon drear: no, it is not
> thele – that drive the poifoned point of torturous thought deep
> to my heart! 'tis not thefe that lay me proftrate in the duft, and
> drive in fobs full floods of tears from my eyes! no, it is the calls
> of an accufing confcience, of bafe ingratitude towards God…
> Oh! my Amy, oh! my wife! and is this bitter, with the bittereft
> mind, that I muft Iofe thy heavenly company and confolation
> foothing? Oh, the dreadful thought does wound and itab to }
> Keeneft quick my buriting heart. I have undone thee; and when
> I look upon the mighty ruin I have pluck'd, pluck'd inftant on
> thy head, oh! where can chearful neis be found: mine muit be
> mourning ever. Oh! my wife! I have undone thee. What the

infuriate hand of foes vindiétive could not have atchieved, in mercy would not, I have wrought. Thy hufband — thy hufband loved with fuch unfhaken truth. — Thy hufband loved with fuch afteady flame. — Even he hath on thee pluck'd, on thee, his foul's companion and life's beft friend, fuch defolation as, to view, would draw from the wild favage, pity's deepeft groan... Thou that is innocent of everything but that laft unfortunate affair; but the ungrateful wretches that were in the room along with me, have told the juttices, that thou brought the faws in, tied to thy thigh. Oh! the bafe, lying wretches, for thou neither brought them, nor ever did know that we had fuch inftruments. Haq the bafe wretches laid the whole charge upon me, I could have borne it and forgiven them, and every enemy I have upon earth. The Lord grant I may meet with the fame forgivenefs and mercy from God.

Edward Miles

In 1791 Edward Miles, his brother George Miles, and their brother-in-law Edward Lydgate, robbed the mail from Warrington to Manchester. Details are sparse about what happened during this crime but in January of 1792 a 'hue and cry' was issued from the police, Bow Street, London, for the apprehension of these three men in connection to the robbery and the murder of the mail boy. A reward of £200 was issued by the post office, a hefty sum for the time. In July of that year a man named Whiteman was arrested and held at Launceston gaol in connection with the crime, but this doesn't seem to have come to anything and in June of 1793, Edward Miles was finally arrested in Manchester.

The post boy, James Hogwarth, was killed brutally and his body dumped in a river. He was found with stabs to his throat and a bruised eye. He left behind him a heavily pregnant wife. There is no further mention of George Miles and Edward Lydgate and it seems Edward Miles alone took the fall. Whether this was because he was indeed the one who carried out the murder, or whether he was simply the only one of the three who could be found, Edward Miles was executed and his body hung in chains on the Manchester Road near where the crime was committed. In 1845 Edward Miles's gibbet irons were unearthed at the site of the crime. Today the

Signpost at Stoney Middleton, Derbyshire, showing the way to Black Harry Gate where the highwayman Black Harry operated. (Photo by author)

A view from the bottom of Black Harry Lane in the Peak District where the highwayman, Black Harry operated. (Photo by author)

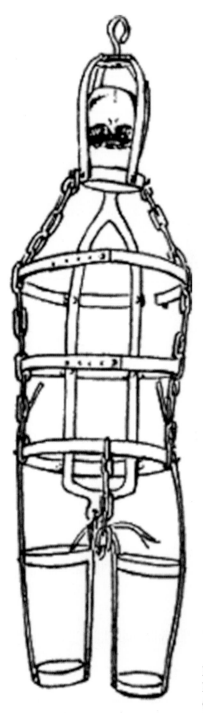

Photo of illustration from Albert Hartshorne's book, *Hanging In Chains*, depicting the gibbet cage of John Bread. (Photo and book in the public domain)

The following most pathetic and affecting letter was written by Spence Broughton to his Wife the night before his Execution

April 14th 1792 York Castle

My Dear Eliza

This is the last epistle thou will ever receive from my hand a hand that trembles at the approaching dissolution, so soon so very soon to ensure before thou will open this last epistle of thy unfortunate Husband these eyes which overflow with Tears of Contrition shall have ceased to weep and this heart now fluttering on the verge of eternity shall beat no more. I have prepared my mind to meet death without terror and how happy had that death been the common visitation of Nature. Be not discomforted ... to your friend ... the solitude of my Cell ... taught him, his Spirit hath supported me I have assisted me in my prayers and many a time the moments remorseful anguish whispered peace for my dear Eliza. I never added cruelty to injustice. Yet though I have resolved to meet death without fear, one part of my awful sentence aggravated by being merited chills me with horror when I reflect that my poor remains the Tokens of mortality must not sleep in peace but be buffeted about by the storms of Heaven or parched by the summer's sun which the Traveller shrinks from with disgust and terror: this consideration freezes my Blood, this till this awful gloom these irons yet death itself is not so grievous. Why should I continue to sport with the wretched ... life is at an end. My Eliza my Friend ... the last sad scene approaches when I shall be no more when I shall leave the World and ... dear to its Mercy and not only thee but my unprotected children the pledges of love: through misfortune, through dissipation, through vice and infamy on my part, uncharged Fool that I ... think Friendship could exist but with virtue: If I had listened to the advice thou hast given me we had been a happy Family, respectable and respected; but it is past that advice ... hath been slighted, I am doomed to an ignominious death, and thou and my Children to want ... brought to infamy. To thee alone I trust the education of those ill fated Creatures when ... more than ever love and weep for, to warn him to avoid gaming, of every description ... awful vice which has caused their father to be suspended a long and lasting spectacle to the Eye of curiosity. Teach them the ways of Religion in their early Years, cause them to ... some Trade that Business may fill their minds and leave no room for dissipation; ... ted round your Winters Fire, when the little Innocents enquire after their unfortunate ... tell them gaming was his ruin; neglected all religious duties; he never conversed with ... solitude; he stifled the upbraidings of conscience in the Company of wicked and profligate companions; and is hung on high a sad and dismal ... after times. I ... us employed while Tears trickle down my Face, I have so ill deserved ... these and Eyes pleasant would death be to me on a sick Bed after my Soul had made ... with God, with God I hope its peace is made, he is not a God all terror but a God of Mercy I rely and on the Interposition of a Saviour may my Tears my penitance and deep ... acceptable to that almighty being before whom I am so shortly to appear, once more Eliza ad[ieu] ... Pen falls from my hand and slumber overtakes me the next will be the sleep of death

Spence Brough[ton]

Spence Broughton's last letter to his wife from prison, held in store at Sheffield Museums. (Photo by author with kind permission from Sheffield Museums)

The tower at Lincoln Castle named Cobb Hall, where public hangings took place before bodies were then transported to their gibbets. (Photo by author)

Replica of the double gibbet used to display the only woman known to have been gibbeted in Britain, Dorothy Newman. (Photo by Andy Malbon, permission by Creative Commons licensing)

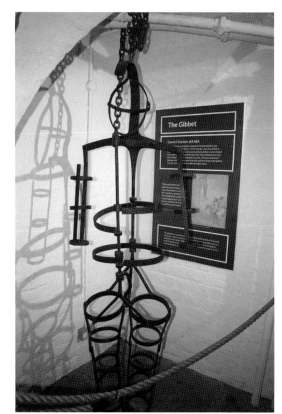

Right: The complete body irons made for the last man gibbeted in Britain, James Cook, on display at Nottingham's Museum of Crime and Justice. (Photo by author)

Below: The yew tree at Darby Green, Hampshire, from which the highwayman, Parson Darby, was hung. (Photo by author)

Above: Neolithic mound in the Peak District where Anthony Lingard, the last man gibbeted in Derbyshire, was hung in chains. (Photo by author)

Left: Rembrandts's study of the female murderer, executed and then displayed on a gibbet in Holland. (Photo and image in the public domain)

Sketch of a gibbet by the artist T. Bewick. (Photo and image in the public domain)

Above: Sketch of a
double gibbeting by
the artist Harper, 1895.
(Photo and image in the
public domain)

Right: Post and plaque
at the spot where the
thief Jack Upperton was
gibbeted, stating J U 1774.
(Photo by Simon Carey
and permission by Creative
Commons licensing)

CONFESSION:

With a short account of the life and behavior of that wicked and barbarous murderer

JOHN KEALE;

Both before, at, and after his trial and condemnation, at the Lent Assize in the County Hall of Lincoln, on Tuesday the 7th of March, 1731, by the Lord Baron *Page*, by whom he was deservedly condemned to be Gibbeted alive for a most horrid and bloody murder committed on the body of his wife and young child in September last.

In which is likewise contained a relation how the instigation of the devil he was tempted and brought upon through an outrageous and furious jealousy with the melancholy apprehensions of poverty and want, to massacre his family in such an inhuman manner, drawing down the just judgment of heaven upon himself, for such an unpardonable villainy as is shocking to all mankind, and is scarce to be paralled in History.

The heads of a Sermon preached on that occasion.

Math. xix, 18 *Jesus saith, thou shalt do no murder.*

Numb. xxxv. 16. *If he smite with an instrument of iron so that he die, he is a murderer: a murderer shall surely be put to death.*

A pamphlet published after the gibbeting of John Keale for the murder of his wife and child, detailing the crime and trial. The pamphlet was gifted to Lincoln Library in 1900 where it is still kept. (Photo by kind permission of Lincoln Library)

Right: The gibbet cage of John Keale, on display at Louth Museum. (Photo by kind permission of Louth Museum)

Below: The label on the tobacco box made from Ralph Smith's gibbet post, reading, 'Box made from wood Ralph Smith's Gibbet near the London Road'. (Photo by kind permission of the Boston Guildhall Museum)

The tower at Lincoln Castle named Lucy's Tower, where private hangings took place once public execution had been abolished. (Photo by author)

The calling card of executioner William Marwood who operated at Lincoln Castle and invented the 'long drop' method of hanging. (Photo by kind permission of the Boston Guildhall Museum)

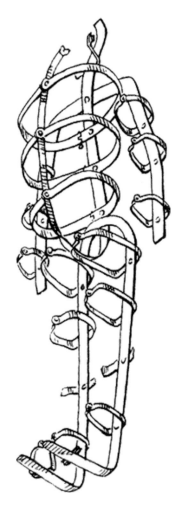

Right: Sketch of Edward Miles's gibbet cage which is on display in Warrington Museum, from the book 'Obsolete Punishments' by C. Madely. (Photo and image in the public domain)

Below: Pub in Sheffield named after the spot where Spence Broughton was gibbeted. (Photo by author)

Left: Remains of the original gibbet post in Suffolk, used to gibbet Jonah Snell in 1698. (Photo by Keith Evans and permission by Creative Commons licensing)

Below: Roadside plaque in Frampton, Lincolnshire, at the spot where Ralph Smith was gibbeted. (Photo by author)

THE GIBBET PIT

ON THIS SITE IN 1792 STOOD THE GIBBET ON WHICH HUNG THE BODY OF RALPH SMITH, THE LAST MAN IN THE BOSTON AREA TO BE HUNG IN CHAINS. HE WAS ACCUSED OF THE MURDER OF GENTLE SUTTON.

ERECTED BY FRAMPTON PARISH COUNCIL APRIL 1983

The head irons used to gibbet Ralph Smith. Kind permission by the Boston Guildhall Museum.

The tobacco box made from Ralph Smith's gibbet post. (Photo by kind permission of the Boston Guildhall Museum)

Above: Information plaque standing next to the Smugglers Stone, which details the case, crimes and punishments of the Hawkhurst Gang and records the original text on the stone, which has now worn away. (Photo by Emily Jessica Turner, with kind permission)

Left: A commemorative stone erected in Chichester in 1749 at the site of the hanging of three members of the Hawkhurst Gang that same year. (Photo by Emily Jessica Turner, with kind permission)

Sketch of a gibbeted pirate from Albert Hartshorne's book *Hanging In Chains*, 1891.
(Book and photo in the public domain)

Blacksmith's shop owned by the murderer Tom Lee in Grassington, Yorkshire. (Photo by Pauline E and permission by Creative Commons licensing)

Above left: The head-irons used on Tom Otter gibbeted near Lincoln, head irons now on display at Doddington Hall. (Photo by author)

Above right: Replica of the gibbet William Winter was gibbeted on in Northumberland in 1792. (Photo by Russel Wils and permission by Creative Commons licensing) irons are on display in Warrington Museum, minus the head irons. It's said that when the gibbet was found it still contained Edward's skull, as gibbets often did, the skull being the one part of the skeleton that couldn't fall through the irons or be easily removed. If this is true and the head irons are missing, this was likely taken as a souvenir or curiosity by some individual, but unfortunately the whereabouts of this are not known today.

Pirates

> To Execution Dock, I must go, I must go,
> To Execution Dock, I must go,
> To Execution dock will many thousands flock,
> But I must bear the shock and must die.

From The Dying Words of Captain Robert Kidd.

Execution Dock was placed on the shoreline of the River Thames at Wapping, London, and was used for executing pirates for more than 400 years. This was used for smugglers and mutineers sentenced to death by the admiralty courts, and it was also used to afterwards enact forms of post-mortem punishment. It's hard to imagine what this place would have looked and smelled like for anyone living or working nearby, or simply for anyone passing through. The spectacle of the gallows and of gibbeted pirates swinging by the side of the river must have been appalling, and it does seem to have put fear into the hearts of many smugglers on the seas. Though it's worth noting, as with most other public executions and gibbeting, this area was packed with eager onlookers and death tourists.

The exact location of the gallows at Execution Dock is uncertain, but by the Prospect of Whitby pub there now stands a replica gibbet post and noose. It could have been the site of Execution Dock and it certainly is in the right area. Some say if you look closely an 'E' marks the spot on the Sun Wharf Building and this is where the executions took place. Others mark it as where Wapping station now stands. Not surprisingly many businesses would like to lay claim to their building standing where this grisly landmark once was. The Captain Kidd pub holds the name of one of the most famous pirates executed here and afterwards hung in chains, but the Town of Ramsgate pub is probably where this actually happened.

There has been a pub standing on this site since the 1400s, originally called The Hostel and then The Red Cow. It was named Ramsgate Old Town in 1766 before being renamed the Town of Ramsgate in 1811. Behind the pub, Wapping Old Stairs descend towards the river and it's here that pirates were once tied to a post and left to drown at high tide, an eerie form of slow execution and torture reserved for these criminals of the high seas. The post is still there today. Perhaps because of this touchable link to punishing pirates, this is thought to be a high contender for the location of Execution Dock, but all we have is a jigsaw puzzle with lots of pieces missing, so we can never be sure.

Execution Dock was used mostly to execute pirates, by hanging and by drowning and often by both. Captured pirates were subject to some of the most extreme forms of public execution and post-mortem punishment, not because it was extra brutal but because it seemed necessary to kill them over and over, and to display their bodies in the most gruesome fashion. Not all pirates were dealt with in the same way, but chaining them to the post behind the Town of Ramsgate was a popular and fitting end to their thieving lives. They had operated their criminal activities on the sea, so they should die in the sea. This may have been an early form of execution that fell under the 'eye for an eye' way of doing things, but as a tradition, just like gibbeting, it continued long after it was considered an inhumane way to dispose of these men. Once the switch was made to hanging publicly at the dock, the tradition of chaining them to the post and letting the sea deal with them continued, just as gibbeting continued after hanging. Pirates were hanged by the neck until dead, but this was purposefully a slow process. Hanging for pirates involved a short drop, which meant the men didn't experience a quick death; a short drop meant the criminals suffered a slow and painful death of strangulation, rather than their spinal column being snapped at the neck by a long drop. Even this wasn't enough and pirates were then chained to the post and left there until three tides had covered them.

This symbolic way of allowing the sea to consume them became a ritual. It served no purpose other than continuing the 'eye for an eye' mentality and perhaps as a warning to other pirates, but it was most likely done simply because it was a traditional practice. This was how pirates had always been dealt with. It was poetic justice. The bodies of most pirates were then sent to the surgeon for dissection, but the most notorious or bloodthirsty pirates needed even further punishment and a public display of justice. The bodies of these pirates were tarred and hung in chains by the very sea they had used for their criminal activities. So, only the most brutal and prolific pirates were treated to this exceptional punishment? No, as with most of the history of justice and post-mortem punishments, who received extra punishment and who didn't is inconsistent and often confusing. It does seem to have been the most famous pirates who were given this extra send off, and perhaps that has more to do with perceived justice and as a warning to others.

William Kidd

Captain William Kidd from Greenock on the Clyde, Scotland, had a long and successful career as a captain in the British service, sailing wherever his commission took him, often to deal with unruly natives who disrupted British movements. The line between privateer and pirate is a blurry one and it is hard to say when he was acting under official British orders and when he was not. He was certainly on an official mission under orders from the British government to suppress pirate behaviour in the Indian ocean in 1696 when things got sticky. It seems William took some matters into his own hands when his crew began a mutiny. He dealt with his mutinous crew, killing at least one of them in a vicious attack, then stole a ship, and sailed to the West Indies. This was pirate behaviour and on his arrival he was arrested and sent back to Britain in 1699.

If William Kidd thought his service to the British government and his friends in high places would help him at this point, he was wrong. He was in his mid-fifties, a pirate, and he was sentenced to death for his crimes. But Captain Kidd wasn't one to go out without some flair. He was hanged with other members of his crew but while they dutifully died, Kidd's rope snapped and he was left confused and alive on the ground. The executioner swiftly hoisted him back up and this time he hanged until he was dead. The crowd were shocked, by all accounts, but also fascinated and saw this as a further amusement and also perhaps an attempt by Kidd to escape his death, maybe they even thought the devil had a hand in it. Kidd was drunk when he went to the gallows so the whole thing was something of a farce. Kidd was then chained to the post and the customary three tides washed over him. From there his alcohol-riddled body, damaged by the rope and beaten by the waves, was taken to Tilbury Point on the lower reaches of the Thames; he was hung in chains for everyone to see and to remember what happens to treacherous pirates.

John Gow

John Gow from the Orkney Islands felt the lure of the sea from an early age, but he never intended on being a pirate. He sailed as crew to Santa Cruz, but when the conditions on board the ship became intolerable he and other crew members mutinied. Gow was a natural leader and soon took charge of the situation, murdering the captain and taking over command of the ship. On his return to Scotland he passed himself off as a wealthy man, which technically he was now, and assumed a new name. But when one of his former crew members handed himself in, Gow's name came up as the orchestrater of the mutiny and he was soon found out. He was sentenced to hang at Execution Dock, but it seems he still had many friends and admirers. On his hanging in 1729 it's said that a handful of men rushed forward and pulled at his legs so he would experience a quicker death and wouldn't suffer. The authorities were in no such mood and after his body had been covered by the customary three tides, hung him in chains by the River Thames. John Gow made such an impression on people's minds he was later immortalised by Charles Johnson in *A General History of the Pyrate* and he's also said to be the inspiration for Walter Scott's novel, *The Pirate*.

Captain James Lowry

Captain James Lowry from Scotland appears to have had little trouble in his career as ships' captain until one strange incident took place in 1751 aboard *The Molly*. Ten members of Lowry's crew put an advert in the newspaper calling for Lowry's arrest on account of him mistreating them while out at sea and murdering one Kenneth Hossack, foremast man. The complaints against him by his crew included him breaking the jaw bone of William Dwight and fracturing the skull of William Wham. But the charge that brought him to arrest and sentencing was for the death of Kenneth Hossack. The other crew members stated that Hossack was sober and hard working, but that Lowry took a dislike to him and being such a cruel man, tied him up and whipped him until he was dead. In February of 1752 Lowry was arrested and charged with the murder and sentenced to death. On 25 March he was taken from the gaol to the gallows and, when faced with what was about to happen to him, he turned pale and was visibly shocked. Lowry was hung at Execution Dock, his body hanging for twenty minutes until he was certainly dead. Then he was taken by boat to Blackwall where he was hung in chains overlooking the water on which he had committed his crimes.

Punishments for those found guilty of piracy seem so wildly inconsistent it's worth taking a look at how they were sentenced. If they chose to, the Admiralty courts who dealt with all crimes committed at sea could try, sentence, and carry out punishments at sea, and they often did. In 1812, long after pirates had suffered hanging, the three tides, and then tarring and gibbeting, a group of mutineers aboard a British ship, the *Salvador Del Mundo*, were dealt with at sea. Williams (English), Millington (Irish), Joacxhim (Portuguese), and Martin (simply recorded as 'a black'), were all hanged from the yardarm of a vessel of war. A particularly flamboyant spectacle and a very dramatic execution. An eye for an eye? Apart from this being some poetic justice and a show of Admiralty strength, it was also a good way of dealing with prisoners of varying nationalities, as these four were. Most British ships contained a crew from a wide range of countries and dealing with them all back in Britain could have proved problematic. Many Caribbean pirates were caught, sentenced, and executed at sea, never having travelled to shore to receive their justice. This ruled out gibbeting. For those pirates who were either caught back in Britain or were caught and then brought back, the gibbet often awaited them.

Chapter 5

That's Entertainment

When Charles Dickens visited a public hanging in 1849 and talked of the carnival atmosphere, the stalls, the prostitutes, the ruffians, all looking to make a penny from the misfortune of the murdered and the murderers on the gallows, he was clearly appalled. This was the public hanging of Marie and Frederick Manning who had murdered Patrick O'Conner for his fortune.

From Charles Dickens's letter to *The Times*, November, 1849:

> I believe that a sight so inconceivably awful as the wickedness and levity of the immense crowd collected at that execution this morning could be imagined by no man, and could be presented in no heathen land under the sun. The horrors of the gibbet and of the crime which brought the wretched murderers to it faded in my mind before the atrocious bearing, looks, and language of the assembled spectators. When I came upon the scene at midnight, the shrillness of the cries and howls that were raised from time to time, denoting that they came from a concourse of boys and girls already assembled in the best places, made my blood run cold. As the night went on, screeching, and laughing, and yelling in strong chorus of parodies on negro melodies, with substitutions of 'Mrs. Manning' for 'Susannah' and the like, were added to these. When the day dawned, thieves, low prostitutes, ruffians, and vagabonds of every kind, flocked on to the ground, with every variety of offensive and foul behaviour. Fightings, faintings, whistlings, imitations of Punch, brutal jokes, tumultuous demonstrations of indecent delight when swooning women were dragged out of the crowd by the police, with their dresses disordered, gave a new zest to the general entertainment.

When the sun rose brightly—as it did—it gilded thousands upon thousands of upturned faces, so inexpressibly odious in their brutal mirth or callousness, that a man had cause to feel ashamed of the shape he wore, and to shrink from himself, as fashioned in the image of the Devil. When the two miserable creatures who attracted all this ghastly sight about them were turned quivering into the air, there was no more emotion, no more pity, no more thought that two immortal souls had gone to judgement, no more restraint in any of the previous obscenities, than if the name of Christ had never been heard in this world, and there were no belief among men but that they perished like the beasts.

The kind of behaviour witnessed at public hangings might have appalled some people, but public hangings and subsequent gibbetings were big business and attracted vast crowds. Spence Broughton's gibbet is said to have been a magnet for tens of thousands of tourists and in the end was the reason the landowner, tired of crowds trampling over his fields, took the gibbet down. But while this was a nuisance to some, others saw a way they could make some cash from the unusual spectacle. The double gibbeting at Combe Gibbet was highly irregular and the landlord of the Crown and Garter Inn wasn't one to miss an opportunity to capitalise on such an incredible occurrence. He swiftly named the barn at the back of his pub where the pair had been brought and measured for their irons 'Gibbet Barn', and opened it up to curious visitors who wanted to see the very spot where the two murderers had lain.

Although the authorities, and particularly great intellects of the time, were beginning to find the practice of public hangings and gibbeting distasteful and not in keeping with a civilised society, the general public had no such sensibilities. Great crowds continued to gather at pubic executions and the last man to be gibbeted in Britain, James Cook, drew crowds of 40,000 people. But why were we as a people so eager to watch others suffer, and why did we turn such events into celebrations? British people have a strange relationship with death. We are fascinated by it and appalled by it, we treat it with distance and with familiarity. We turn to humour to cover our discomfort and we stare at it while thanking the Lord it is that person dead and not us. There is something of this in attending public hangings and gibbetings. This gives us the chance to reassure ourselves that this is not happening to us – and it won't happen to us because we are not evil criminals. It puts space between ourselves and the barbarity of murderers. And we also have a particular hunger for retribution.

The Case of John Clifton

Cutthroat Lane in Yaxham, Norfolk, had already been named after a murder by the time John Clifton committed his crime there. A young woman's throat was cut here in a brutal murder, and the lane was named after the event, but that was long before John Clifton arrived on the scene. In 1785 Peter and Henry Seaman had been drinking in a nearby pub when they made their way home up Cutthroat Lane. The lane is quiet and bends around sharply, making it the perfect place to hide if you wanted to rob someone on their way home from the pub. And this is exactly what John Clifton did that night. He waited and then sprang out on the two drunk men, knocking them to the ground and robbing them. Peter was fatally wounded in the attack, but lived just long enough to corroborate his brother's testimony and name Clifton as the attacker. Clifton was arrested and sentenced to death for murder. He was executed at Norwich Castle and then his body taken in chains back to Cutthroat Lane to hang on the gibbet. Whether it was the rarity of such a case and spectacle, or whether it had something to do with the famous murderers lane now being used twice for such a crime, the people of the community and neighbouring communities were excited and fascinated by what was going on.

The Norwich Mercury recorded the events at the time:

> Hundreds of the country people came to see the ghastly spectacle, and the result was that for many weeks the vicinity resembled a fair, on Sundays particularly, booths were erected for the sale of drink, and there were some very hilarious scenes.

and years later:

> The remains hung for 25 years ... schoolboys used the corpse as a target, and boasted that they had 'chipped a piece off Cliften'.

Even after the fair had died down and moved on, the fascination with the murderer and his crime continued. When the field next to Cutthroat Lane was ploughed years later, John Clifton's skull was discovered, although there is no mention of the gibbet irons. The man who had murdered Peter Seaman on his way home from the pub that night was now a local legend. Villagers gathered at the scene and it's said the skull was passed around from person to person, each examining it and gazing at it in wonder.

In Norwich Castle Museum today there is kept a fragment of head irons unknown. This piece of a gibbet is a tantalising mystery as there is no record of who it was used for, or how it came to be at the museum. Some say it could have been from the head cage of John Clifton, unearthed when the field was ploughed, but it could just have easily belonged to the numerous other criminals who were hung in chains in Norfolk. It's interesting that only this piece of the gibbet survived and it could well have been found when the earth in the field next to Cutthroat Lane was turned over. The fragment was only catalogued by the museum in 1999 and its life before that remains unknown.

When the travel company Thomas Cook first began in Leicester in 1841, they offered day trips by coach to public hangings, such was the desire of ordinary people to travel distances to witness this incredible spectacle. The riverside inns at Blackwall, London, had spyglasses fixed to their windows so that guests could comfortably sit and gaze out over the water at gibbeted pirates and other criminals hanging there. Greenwich pensioners would sit on their hill with telescopes idly picking out the pirates hanging in chains opposite them on the Isle of Dogs. Newspapers from the time tell of the outcry by tourists and residents when the gibbets were removed, depriving them of their amusement.

There was also a certain entertainment to be had from gathering souvenirs and keepsakes from gibbets. People were doing this almost as soon as a gibbet went up, and over the years it was standing parts of the post and even the bones themselves would disappear. When gibbets were dismantled eager souvenir hunters would assemble and take whatever they could. Posts were often used for nearby farm gates and fences and sometimes the wooden posts, parts of the irons, and the bones of the gibbeted men, were turned into usable items. Ralph Smith's post was used to make a tobacco box. This was in the possession of G.E. Hackford, born 1865, until he gifted the item to Boston Guildhall Museum where it is on display today. Hackford had a curiosity shop, full of unusual collectable items and it seems the more macabre the curiosity the better. John Keale's gibbet post was used to make a small wooden box which Louth Museum have a photo of. The box even has an inscription on paper inside which reads, partially legible: 'This box is made from ... of the post on ... John Keal ... in chains near ... for the murder ... wife ... in the year 1731.' Unfortunately the whereabouts of the box now are unknown.

Anthony Lingard's irons were made into toasting forks and his skull has been passed around various private collectors and exhibitions. Eugene Aram's skull was much sought after as a curiosity, and was of especial interest to phrenologists of the time who believed that the size and shape of the skull could determine a person's personality and was a direct relationship to what was going on in the mind. His skull was studied under this 'science' to try and better understand how a man of such intellect could do something so terrible. Andrew Mill's gibbet was dismantled bit by bit by locals who believed it had magical properties, and in particular could cure a toothache. Tom Otter's irons were said to have been made into a nutcracker and the item is held at the North Lincolnshire Museum now. When Tom Otter's gibbet was blown down in a storm and it was decided it was time to let it stay down, Edwin Jarvis the owner of nearby Doddington Hall, walked out to view the spectacle with some curiosity. It's said the constable at the scene took some of the irons, and when Jarvis asked if he could have the prized head irons, his request was granted. Tom Otter's head irons are still on display in Doddington Hall, sitting on the mantlepiece in the dining room, opposite an equally gruesome scold's bridle.

So, why did we hold these items in such regard, consider them souvenirs, and in some way charmed? These things were part of the post-mortem punishment for murderers. If anything, you'd think we would see them as being cursed or haunted, or at least in some way attached to evil. Why did we instead attach this positive superstition and care to them? Why did we want them incorporated into our everyday lives and kept as curiosities? Our preoccupation with death, grisly punishments, and murder, has never gone away and it seems the more shocking a tale of murder is the more we feed on it. It is a form of entertainment, as is murder itself.

The Congleton Cannibal, Samuel Thorley

The wonderful *Magazine and Extraordinary Museum*, published in 1808 by Archibauld Press, relates a most shocking and unthinkable murder due to a most shocking and unthinkable desire – the want of human flesh. No, not sexual desires, but culinary desires, Samuel Thorley was the Congleton Cannibal. There's no evidence to suggest he had ever done anything like this before, but it seems Samuel took a liking to Anne Smith, a ballad singer, and he wanted to do more than listen to her sing. Samuel wanted to eat her. It's not known whether he targeted her specifically because she was famous in the area, or if she was simply in the wrong place at the wrong time. The year was 1776 and Anne was just 22 when Samuel saw her walking near Congleton. He persuaded her to walk a little further with him until they were in a more secluded spot and there Samuel began his butchery.

Samuel dismembered Anne and then removed her tongue and bowels. He sliced the fleshy parts of her body away from her and these alone he kept, doing his best to discard all other parts of poor Anne. He took these cuts of meat back to his lodgings and asked his landlady to cook them, telling her it was pork. Samuel then attempted to eat Anne, but apparently he found the meat didn't agree with him and he threw it out. The remains of Anne Smith were found the next day by two men walking cattle. It seems that although Samuel hadn't displayed any signs of mental health issues or violence before, he was instantly suspected because he worked as a butcher and had been acting strangely in the town when the murder was mentioned.

Thorley confessed when the meat found at his lodgings was confirmed by a surgeon to be human. His horrified landlady was about to cook the prized 'pork' for her and her daughter, not wanting to see it go to waste. When Samuel was asked why he had done it, he replied that he'd heard human flesh tasted like pork and he wanted to find out if it was true. He was executed on 11 April 1777 and afterwards hung in chains on the heath near Congleton, where the horrendous murder had taken place. A witness at the trial said he had never seen any sign of insanity in Thorley and that he was convinced the man had done this purely out of greed. In 1876 *The Leek Times* published the diary of the Rev. Jonathan Wilson, Master of Congleton Grammar School and Vicar of Biddulph, to mark the 100 year anniversary of this most terrible crime.

Saturday 23rd November 1776 While at dinner heard of a most abominable murder a woman cut into a score of pieces in Prester Fields Brook.

Sunday 24th November 1776 The murderer detected and lodged in the town hall.

Monday 25th November 1776 Sam Thorley the murderer sent to Chester.

Thursday 11th April 1777 At school after dinner the boys are given leave to go and see Sam Thorley drawn on the gibbet.

Gibbetings, like public hangings, were thought of as perfectly fine events and spectacles for children to attend and view. At William Saville's public hanging in 1844 outside the County Hall, Nottingham, the crowd was reportedly huge and totally unmanageable. The crushing as people jostled for position and a better view of the entertainment meant some were fainting. At 8 am William was led to the gallows outside the Shire Hall where the crowd had gathered. He was hanged, but something happened as the drop opened and the crowd began to panic. We don't know what caused people to be spooked like this, but suddenly everyone was desperate to get out of there. In the chaos that followed many were trampled in the stampede. Twelve people died and over a hundred were injured. If we look at the ages of those who lost their lives that day we can see that this day out at the gallows was perfectly acceptable for children to attend.

Mary Stevenson aged 23
James Fisher aged 22
Milicent Shaw aged 20
Eliza Smithhurst aged 19
John Bednell aged 14
James Marshall aged 14
Eliza Percival aged 13
Eliza Hannah Shuttleworth aged 12
Susannah Smedley aged 14
Thomas Watson aged 14
Mary Easthope aged 14
Thomas Easthope aged 9

But while crowds thronged to hangings and carnivals were set up around gibbets, there was some disgust, as we see from Charles Dickens above. Booths were set up, stalls arranged, prostitutes attended looking for business, fortune tellers and entertainers arrived and the whole thing was turned into a circus. Although in some cases, like Spence Broughton, where crowds of tourists continued to make the journey to view the gibbet years after it had been erected, usually this celebrating was short lived and there was a distinctive difference between the party atmosphere of a fresh gibbeting and coming face to face with the rotting flesh of the corpse of the gibbeted man years or decades later.

From *Legends and Traditions of Huntingdonshire* by W.H. Bernard Saunders 1888:

> Many of the present residents of Alconbury can recollect a tall, gaunt post, which stood beside the Great North Road, near the coppice between Alcon-bury and Brampton Hut, and around which, as boys, they were accustomed to play on summer evenings. The post, which was removed, or fell into decay, about 30 years ago, was known as Matchan's gibbet. Upon it, in the year 1786, was hung in chains the body of Gervase Matchan, who, six years before, had foully murdered a di'ummer boy, Benjamin Jones, on that spot; and who would have escaped the legal penalty of his crime had it not have been for the circumstances related in the following legend, which are mainly extracted from Matchan's confession before the Rev. J. Nicholson, of Great Paxton.

Gervase Matcham did get away with his crime for a while, until his conscience, or the ghost of the drummer boy as he stated, made him confess all. Maybe he would have got away with it completely had he not been driven to near insanity by his guilt. Matcham was a sailor from Yorkshire. In 1786, at the age of 31, he could finally take no more of the guilt that ravaged him. Six years earlier he'd been a private in the 49th foot regiment. Gervase wore the distinctive scarlet red uniform and was trusted enough to accompany the quartermaster's son, Benjamin, to Diddington Hall to collect money for supplies. On their way back, Benjamin's pockets full of gold, Matcham saw his chance at financial freedom. He slit young Benjamin's throat and took off with the money, ditching his red uniform and dressing instead in ordinary clothes. He fled back to York and had apparently got away with the crime. But after Matcham spent all the money he enlisted in the navy and by 1786 he was consumed with guilt over what he had done and told others that he saw the ghost of Benjamin everywhere he went. It's said Matcham went mad and was relieved to finally confess his crime and get the ghost off his back. Gervase Matcham was executed and then hung in chains at the spot where Benjamin's body had been discovered six years earlier. Matcham was dressed in the distinctive scarlet red uniform once more, the material packed around his corpse in the gibbet and flying like a flag of murder from the irons. Cuthbert Bede, the pen name of clergyman Edward Bradley, who died in 1889, wrote in his *Notes and Queries*, an account he had taken from an old local man:

> 'I mind too,' said the old man, 'the last gibbet as ever stood in Huntingdonshire. It was put up on the other side of Alconbury on the Buckden road. Matcham was the man's name. He was a soldier, and had been quartered at Alconbury; and he murdered his companion, who was a drummer boy, for the sake of his money. Matcham's body was hung in chains, close by the road side, and the chains clipped the body and went tight round the neck, and the skull remained a long time after the rest of the body had got decayed. There was a swivel on the top of the head, and the body used to turn about with the wind. It often used to frit me as a lad, and I have seen horses frit with it. The coach and carriage people were always on the look out for it, but it was never to my taste. Oh, yes I can mind it rotting away, bit by bit, and the red rags flapping from it. After a while they took it down, and very pleased I were to see the last of it.'

Coaches of people were, apparently, always looking to see this spectacle and to catch a glimpse of Matcham's red coat. How long this death tourism went on for, we don't know, but for those who had to live close to it, this was a horror they were glad to be rid of. Matcham's gibbet doesn't quite give up entertaining us yet though. As Saunders mentions above, the post remained for a long time and as children, Saunders and his friends used to play around the former gibbet post on summer's evenings.

Those who had travelled to see the gibbet of Gervase Matcham remarked on how unusual it was, being fixed on a beam suspended between two elm trees and a swivel in the middle of the beam from which the gibbet turned this way and that in the wind. This suggests these tourists had seen other gibbets and perhaps were fascinated enough to seek them out.

Much of the behaviour of crowds at gibbetings was bravado, a kind of uneasy 'rather him than me' attitude, and as we are British, humour was often used to dispel any fear or nervousness about the situation. There are a handful of stories of jokes being played and people being dared to visit a remote gibbet by themselves, only to find that when they address the corpse hanging there, someone they knew in life, there is a ghostly reply. The pranksters in these cases were hidden from view and saw the whole thing as a laugh, scaring the daylights out of the poor person who was the butt of the joke. Sometimes at the erection of gibbets and the party that went on around it, visitors tried to climb the gibbet and interfere with the irons and corpse, placing items on the bodies for fun. It's ironic that the post-mortem punishment that was supposed to act as a deterrent was often used as an excuse for a party and was treated as a fun day out and ended up being some kind of festival.

Chapter 6

The Gibbet as a Landmark

Imagine the rusty creaking irons, squeaking as they sway in the wind, the birds huddled at the flesh of the corpse inside them. Imagine this long term signpost is on your regular route, your daily commute. Imagine this macabre landmark is there for so long it becomes something you grow used to. You may still be aware of the terrible stench wafting from the decaying flesh, the rattle of the bones as the skin and muscles finally leave the irons and the skeleton is all that's left, but it has been there so long, it just is.

We can find references to gibbets from popular literature of the time that tell us they were semi-permanent fixtures in our landscape. These writings tell us that gibbets were used as markers for roads and travel routes, as grisly reminders of shocking crimes, like a monument to that slice of history, and as a thing of terror. People who lived nearby often avoided walking on the road where they knew the gibbet stood and would find alternative routes. Very few people walked on Ralph's Lane if they could help it while the gibbet stood there, afraid of his ghost and also afraid of coming face to face with the decaying murderer.

In Mrs Sherwood's *The Fairchild Family* published 1818, Mr Fairchild seeks to teach his children, aged 6–9, a lesson about being argumentative and naughty. He takes them to Blackwood, where he knows the body of a murderer hangs on the gibbet in irons. He picks out this spot and he makes the children view the corpse as a warning to behave themselves. This was written at a time when gibbets were a part of our landscape and were often used as landmarks. The gibbet could be in its position for decades and would have been a well known fixture. In part two of the book, the boy Henry goes back along the same route and remarks on the absence of the gibbet now. This once steady landmark has been dismantled after years of standing, but even though the gibbet is now gone, the memory of it remains.

Criminals were hung in gibbets partly as a warning and although they were hung as close to the scene of the crime as possible, the location chosen was often picked for its maximum impact on travellers and passers-by as well. The haunting spectacle of the swinging gibbet cage was often purposefully placed by highways or on hills to dominate the landscape. Imagine then, a member of your own family committed some terrible act (or didn't), was executed and their body brought back to the scene of the crime, and hung in chains, their corpse swinging in the wind for years and years as it decomposed, the awful stench carrying on the breeze and invading your home and everywhere you went. Imagine you had to pass their lifeless decaying body each day as you walked along the lane. In the case of John Walford this is exactly what happened. Walford's body was hung in chains just a quarter of a mile from his parents' house and directly opposite it, so every time they stepped from their home the first thing they saw was their son's corpse hanging in its gibbet cage.

The bodies of smugglers were gibbeted by the coast as this was as close to their crimes as possible, but it also served as a warning to other smugglers. It was likely other criminals of this type would have known the offender and would have to see his body swinging in the salty wind when they made their way down to the rocky shore. But in London, things were sometimes different. Here particularly, gibbets were hung in locations that would have the maximum impact on passers-by, and in some cases this meant multiple bodies were hung in chains at the same location over the years, making the location famous for this spectacle. In the case of the Hawkhurst gang, an infamous band of smugglers, thieves and murderers, there was a predicament. These men were guilty of a range of crimes so hanging them close to the scene of their wrong doings was difficult, and in any case this doesn't seem to be something that was practised in London as it was in the rest of the country. Perhaps because it wasn't possible to hang bodies in chains in the big city, the surrounding area was usually chosen as the best site.

The Hawkhurst Smuggling Gang

The Hawkhurst smugglers were a gang of men who terrorised the coast between Dorset and Kent in the years between 1735 and 1749. It's said their numbers swelled to 500 men at times and they were brutal and vicious. This was not a smuggling gang alone, the Hawkhursts also carried out highway robberies and broke into houses. In short, they were a menace and something had to be done. As time went on the gang was becoming more and more brazen and believing they were untouchable, terrorised the inhabitants of nearby towns, mocked landlords by drinking their fill and refusing to pay, and rampaged, stealing horses and threatening to shoot anyone who tried to stop them. In Goldhurst, however, they met their match. The inhabitants of Goldhurst were so affronted by the behaviour of the Hawkhursts they decided to fight back, and they formed their own militia. War between the two gangs was declared and the Hawkhursts gave the Goldhurst militia a date and time they would meet for battle. This gave the Goldhursts the upper hand as they were on home turf and well prepared. Amazingly, it seems the Goldhursts did prevail and they chased the Hawkhursts back to the sea.

This was the beginning of the end for the Hawkhursts. The tide was turning. Soon after this, buoyed up with confidence and defiance following the recent battle, other members of communities terrorised by the gang started to talk. When an excise man named Galley received information about the smugglers, word got out he was after them, and he was captured by the gang, drugged, tortured and eventually burned alive. It seems this was too much for some members of the gang and at least one of them betrayed the others by informing on them, a risky thing to do as members of such a brutal gang. But it worked. As a result of this Benjamin Tapner, William Carter, Richard Mills, Richard Mills the younger, John Cobby, John Hammond, and William Jackson were all arrested and sentenced to death for their crimes. Their crimes were many, but particularly for the crimes of smuggling, highway robbery and murder, they were sentenced to hanging in chains following execution. Jackson died on the evening of the sentencing, and although it was known he was ill during his trial, it was said to be a death of terror at the prospect of the gibbet, such was the power of this macabre procedure. The rest of the gang who had been captured were hanged and gibbeted in 1749. The locations chosen for their gibbets are interesting, as they seem to have been chosen more as a warning to other criminals than we typically see in gibbets in other parts of Britain.

William Carter was gibbeted on the Portsmouth Road, which was the main route from Portsmouth into London. It's likely this location was chosen as a deterrent to any would-be criminals travelling into London. The spectacle of an executed smuggler hanging in chains by the roadside would have been a grim reminder of what happened to those who committed such crimes.

Richard Mills senior, aged 60 at the time of his execution, and Richard Mills junior, aged 30, were part of a prolific smuggling family, including son John Mills who was also part of the gang but wasn't apprehended. The pair were hardened criminals, known to be of bad character in their community and at their trial they declared they had been doing this for years and didn't see anything wrong with it. Their gibbets were hung in prominent locations at Chichester.

Benjamin Tapner, aged around 30 at the time of his execution, pleaded guilty to his crimes but also cited the devil as having 'got hold of' him. He stated that he was persuaded by others to become a smuggler and claimed it was the bad company he'd fallen into that had made him do such terrible things. He was hung in chains at Rook's Hill near Chichester.

John Hammond and John Cobby were gibbeted together on Selsey Bill. This location was chosen specifically as a warning to other smugglers, who were known to operate from this headland and who were accomplices or known acquaintances of the gang. The exact location of the gibbet isn't known and has probably been swept out to sea by now, but a blue plaque is displayed on Selsey Bill that remembers the gruesome spectacle on the coast line.

> Gibbet Field. as a warning to others the bodies of two smugglers executed in 1749 were hung in chains from the gibbet that stood in this field, much of which is now under the sea.

William Jackson escaped the gibbet and was buried hastily, but his part in the terrible crimes of the Hawkhurst gang were not forgotten. The Smugglers Stone, on the Broyle Road in Chichester, marks the spot where Jackson was buried. It is weather beaten and difficult to make out these days, but an information board next to it gives us the words chiselled into the stone:

> Near this place was buried the body of William Jackson, a proscribed smuggler, who upon a special commission

of oyer and terminer held at Chichester on the 16th day of January 1748–9 was, with William Carter, attained for the murder of William Galley, a custom house officer and who likewise was together with Benjamin Tapner, John Cobby, John Hammond, Richard Mills the elder and Richard Mills the younger, his son, attained for the murder of Daniel Chater. But dying in a few hours after sentence of death was pronounced upon him he thereby escaped the punishment which the heinousness of his complicated crimes deserved and which was the next day most justly inflicted upon his accomplices. As a memorial to posterity and a warning to this and succeeding generations this stone is erected A.D. 1749.

William Fairall escaped being captured for the murders of William Carter and William Galley, crimes he would surely have taken part in, but his run of luck didn't last long and the terrible things he had done didn't stray far from him. He was a marked man and the authorities were after him, and they'd get him on whatever charges they could. He was arrested for smuggling at some point in 1747, but managed to escape. He was surely being tracked and followed because in October of that year, along with other members of the gang, William broke into a customs house in Hampshire to take back the tea they had smuggled and lost. They were soon arrested and although the only charge that was brought against them at this time was the small crime of housebreaking, Fairall was sentenced to death and there after hanging in chains. Although there was no mention at the trial of his other more serious crimes, this career criminal had stacked up enough wrongdoing to see him be made an example of. William Fairall was gibbeted on the village green in Horsmondon, and close by today Gibbet Lane acts as a landmark

Some of the members of the Hawkhurst gang were gibbeted in their home villages and towns and close to where they had lived and where their families still lived, even though this was not where their crimes had taken place. It's hard to say what the reasoning behind this was, it would certainly have been a difficult thing for their families to endure and many of them did attempt to remove the gibbets. Placing gibbets close to where the defendants had lived and where their families still lived was usually done in other parts of Britain because that was where the crimes had been committed. These were small communities and most criminals and murderers stole and killed on their own doorsteps. These were either opportunist thieves or murders of people the defendants knew well. This wasn't the case with the Hawkhursts, so why gibbet them in their own communities? It could be, as with many punishments of the time, that this was simply perceived to be the done thing. Whether it was considered or not, gibbeting criminals in their own villages and towns could be a brutal reminder to their families of the awful crimes, and it could be extremely upsetting for the families of the victims as well. This persistent reminder of the murder of their loved ones seems especially cruel and thoughtless. Something that was often done to show a just punishment fitted the crime may have appeased the wider community, but it only meant prolonged anguish for those closest to the crime.

In Farrington, Lancashire, William Whittle killed his wife and children in 1766. His gibbet was placed 100 yards from his own house where the murders had taken place, and 40 yards from the house of his father-in-law. This meant William's hanging corpse could be seen by his murdered wife's father daily.

Roger Benstead was gibbeted in 1791 after he indirectly murdered Thomas Briggs. Benstead kept cattle on his own land, but when these animals strayed into neighbouring fields it was Thomas Briggs who decided to keep them there in order to teach Benstead a lesson. Benstead at first demanded the release of his cattle to which Briggs replied he could have the animals if he paid a fine for allowing them to stray onto his land. Benstead refused.

Benstead must have been furious because he was soon plotting to murder Briggs for this act, but he wasn't about to get his own hands dirty. Instead he paid a local lad, Thomas Harper, to shoot Briggs, which he did. It's said Briggs crawled some distance before eventually dying from his wounds. The pair were arrested after trying to hide in Undley Hall and they were taken to trial. The boy, Harper, was released but Benstead was sentenced to death and hanging in chains for the plot to murder Briggs. Benstead was gibbeted close to the scene of the crime and also close to the grave of Briggs, whom he had killed. This story and spectacle hung over the village for decades and it's said that as an older man, Thomas Harper still lamented his part in the crime and wished he had also been executed for it. It does seem highly unusual, when looking at other murders like this, plotted by one person and executed by another for payment. It is almost always the murderer themselves who receives the harshest punishment and the mastermind of it who is seen as less culpable. In this case there were obviously wider circumstances that led to this decision. There's no doubt Benstead was an unsavoury character and the true murderer. This report from a newspaper at the time tells of how cruel the man was to a young boy servant. Was this Thomas Harper? Or another boy Benstead had chosen to bully?

From the *Norfolk Chronicle* 1792:

> Whilst the gibbet was preparing for Benstead's body at Lakenheath common, a stripling, who had lived servant with him, was held up to public view with his back bare, and shockingly lacerated by a severe flogging he received from Benstead's son, it had afterwards been rubbed with salt and pork lard, many pieces of which were picked out of the wounds. This piteous spectacle worked up those present into such a pitch of phrenzy, that they could scarcely be restrained from cutting the flesh of the deceased; and had the son been to be found at the moment, it is thought he would have accompanied the father on the same gibbet.

In this case, the placing of the gibbet in the community probably caused most anguish to Harper, the perhaps unwilling murderer who got away with it. It seems he never forgave himself and maybe the sight of the gibbet did cause a change in him.

The story of the gibbet is woven into our history and into our landscape. You don't have to look far to find the word 'gibbet' on street names, place names, areas of land and even pubs. Today you can walk the lane that bears the name of this horrific post-mortem punishment, you can drive along a road and even live in a house that bears the name 'gibbet'. We don't think about it too deeply when we do this, we are doing it every day, but these words branded in our landscape tell of a history we might rather forget. This terrible punishment was used so rarely and sparingly that it always created a lasting impression and the memory of what happened and how it was dealt with stuck to the places where it occurred. Henry Brookman, the case that began our journey through the history of gibbeting, is still with us today. From 1727 right through to our present, the memory of this horrific murder and equally horrific punishment stands as a witness. Henry was gibbeted on Hursley Hill near Bristol, and today a narrow one-lane road snakes through the fields, by Hursley Hill, called Gibbet Lane.

The Case of John Spencer

In the village of Scrooby in Doncaster on 3 July 1779, a terrible double murder took place. This quiet rural village was not used to such terrible deeds and this awful event shook the close community. The tolls in Scrooby were collected by William Yeadon, the toll-booth keeper and on this fateful evening William had been playing cards with John Spencer who was from a nearby village, North Leverton with Habblesthorpe. It just so happened that William's mother, Mary, had visited him this day and was staying over in the toll house with him. John Spencer would have known that William kept the money from the toll in the house and after playing cards there with William he may even have found out where it was.

After leaving on pretence of returning home, Spencer waited until William and Mary had gone to bed and then he returned to the house. It was the early hours of the morning when Spencer broke into the house and attempted to carry away the strongbox that contained the takings from the previous day's toll. Unfortunately he made a racket with the heavy box and William and Mary were disturbed. Alerted by the rattling of coins in the box, the pair soon became aware of what Spencer was doing. But John Spencer had his eye on the money and he wasn't about to let these two get in his way. In a vicious attack he fractured their skulls by repeatedly striking them with a heavy hedge stake, and they both died at the scene. Spencer took the opportunity to go over the rest of the house now, looking for more things he could steal. It was only when he tried to dispose of the bodies by dragging them out of the house and to the River Ryton close by, that passing travellers saw him and alerted the police. He was arrested not once, but twice, after escaping the first arrest and a search party being dispatched to find him. His guilt was in no doubt and he was sentenced to execution and hanging in chains. He was hanged on 16 July at Nottingham and then taken back to Scrooby to be gibbeted close to the toll bar house. It's said he was hung in chains with the hedge stake he had used to commit the murders in his right hand.

This from the *Doncaster Chronicle* describes the effects of the gibbet on the landscape and all those who passed by it or had the misfortune to live near to it:

> After the lapse of a few weeks, a party of soldiers conveyed a deserter passing by the place, the sergeant fired his carbine, loaded with ball, at the corpse, and hit it, which caused a stench, almost unbearable for several days afterwards. The circumstances becoming known, the party was followed, and the sergeant taken, and on being subsequently tried by Court-martial he was found guilty and degraded on the ranks. Years rolled on, and the body gradually became less and less, until nothing was left but the chains which originally shackled it, and these in course of time fell and were secretly conveyed away. For several late years the post, with its withered and weather-beaten arm, was the only vestige left of that deed of blood which sixty-seven years ago filled the minds of the inhabitants of the surrounding districts with horror. But Time, which levels all terrestrial objects with his corroding breath, had for years past been gradually gnarling this once loathing stump to its core, and on the 15th of April 1846 actually accomplished his task, and it fell to rise no more.

John Spencer is remembered not by his name, but by the gibbet. The hill where he was hung in chains is still called Gibbet Hill and the nearby road 'Gibbet Hill Lane' is a residential area. The gibbet post Spencer was hung from was preserved in Doncaster Museum and it was recorded as being there when the museum opened in 1910. The record states '374X part of Scrooby gibbet post, from which John Spencer was hanged in chains for the murder of the Scrooby Toll Bar keeper in 1779.' Unfortunately the post is not locatable now and it's not known what happened to it.

The Case of Sion y Gof

In Powys in Wales, near the village of Llanbrynmair, there is an area of hills and troughs that keep a dark history. Dylife is remote and rolls with a sweeping landscape that was once littered with lead mines.

Further back in history, this was a Roman outpost and has been the site for some interesting archaeological finds. But in 1938 the land here yielded something more grisly than anyone was expecting when a dig uncovered a disturbing relic. This is Gibbet Hill, the place where Sion y Gof was hung in chains. It's thought there was a gallows on this hill from as early as 1700 and it's sometime in the eighteenth century that the terrible double murder occurred here. Some versions of this story say that Sion y Gof was so convinced his wife had been unfaithful to him, he murdered her in a fit of rage, while others have it that Sion y Gof was the one who became involved with another woman and wanted his wife out of the way. Either way, he murdered her and then, realising he wouldn't be able to escape suspicion, he also murdered his daughter and began telling everyone in the village that the pair had left him in order to explain their disappearance. This might have been believed, but the bodies were discovered in a mine shaft where Sion y Gof had thrown them and he was quickly arrested and tried for murder. We don't have much information on the nature of his execution but we do know, as he was the only blacksmith in the village, Sion y Gof had the horrifying task of making his own gibbet irons to fit his own body. It must have been a terrible task. The dig in 1938 uncovered a post pit and further excavations went on to uncover a gibbet iron which still contained the skull of a male. The skull of Sion y Gof, is now on display at The Museum of Wales.

John Massey

The village of Bilstone sits quietly thirteen miles from Leicester, a sleepy suburban place with its fair share of weird tales, hauntings, and folklore. Like many small English villages there is something both charming and unsettling at Bilstone, especially when you encounter the old gibbet post off Gibbet Lane and you realise this hunk of wood that stands cordoned by the side of the road was once used to suspend the dead body of a murderer between heaven and earth. This man was John Massey, an agricultural labourer who lived here in Keeper's Cottage. John's first wife had died some time before and he had remarried and taken on a stepdaughter who was 10 years old. John was a hard man. He drank a lot and he was fond of wrestling and he was well known in the village as someone you would do well to stay on the right side of. His wife, sadly, didn't always manage that. One evening in 1801 John had drunk his fair share in the Curzon Arms at Twycross and he was spoiling for a fight. His wife, Lydia, was his target. Following a violent argument John took hold of his wife and threw her in the mill race where she soon drowned. His stepdaughter had tried to stop him, a big mistake, and she soon followed her mother. However, the mill keeper, on hearing the commotion, stepped in and saved the girl, meaning she was able to give evidence against her vile-tempered step father. Massey was convicted of murder and hanged at Redhill, Birstall, and then his body was transported back to Bilstone the next day where he was hung in a gibbet cage. It's said that John's skeleton was still swinging in the gibbet in 1818 when it was eventually removed. It's not known what happened to John Massey's remains, what was left of him, but the gibbet post has survived and still stands by Gibbet Lane today. It's a weatherworn and embittered piece of wood standing exactly where it always had, the memory of the gibbet cage, John Massey's decaying corpse, and the terrible murder, still eating away at it.

The Case of Anthony Lingard, the Last Man to be Gibbeted in Derbyshire

Wardlow Mires in the Peak District appears as desolate and bleak today as it always has, the land stretching out all around and only a handful of inhabitants to notice. This tiny hamlet near the village of Tideswell has one pub, The Three Stags Heads, and a few old cottages, and only the rolling moorland as far as the eye can see for company. It was in this eerily quiet place that Anthony Lingard became the last man to be gibbeted in Derbyshire in 1815. 21-year-old Anthony had a pregnant girlfriend, Rebecca Nall, and in such a close-knit community there was very little chance of hiding this fact. As Rebecca's body swelled and the baby grew, Anthony knew fingers would be pointed and a swift trip down the aisle would be arranged. But Anthony didn't want to marry Rebecca and become a father, and before his girlfriend started to show Anthony went to some drastic lengths to try and ensure he didn't have to.

It was 15 January 1821 when Anthony Lingard made a life-changing, and history-making, decision. Hannah Oliver, a 70-year-old widow, lived in the toll bar cottage; she was the keeper of the turnpike gate and this could have been why Anthony chose her as his victim, believing she would have money at the cottage. He would have certainly known she lived by herself and probably saw her as an easy target when he cooked up his dark plan. He went to the toll bar cottage on the night of 15 January and broke in. We'll never know if he went there with the intention of doing the old woman harm or if he simply planned to rob her, but before the night was over Anthony had strangled Hannah Oliver to death with a handkerchief and tried to make it look like a suicide. He arranged her body to make it seem as if Hannah had taken her own life – but he hadn't taken into account the evidence of the struggle that Hannah had put up. Her frail old body was covered in bruises and the local constable wasn't fooled for a minute. Anthony had also taken some money and a pair of new red shoes, which would eventually be his downfall.

Wardlow Mires didn't have many suspects to put forward, with such a small population, and it wasn't long before Anthony was on the shortlist, but there was no proof as yet. However, the rumours soon started and as the whispers gathered speed they landed on the ears of the very person who would testify against Anthony. Following the murder, Anthony had visited his pregnant girlfriend, Rebecca, and offered her the red shoes he'd stolen from Hannah Oliver. We can assume he wasn't much of a romantic, and Rebecca was neither fooled nor impressed. Anthony presented her with the shoes, but wanted something in return. She could have the shiny new shoes if she promised to cite another man as the father of her unborn baby, removing him from his responsibilities to her and the child. He could be a free man.

Whatever Anthony's girlfriend said in reply, she was no fool and she refused him. News of Hannah Oliver's death and the break-in would have swept round the village faster than a sneeze and the offended Rebecca went straight to the police and told them about the shoes. Thanks to local cobbler Samuel Marsden, the police were able to identify the missing shoes; Marsden confirmed he had made them and sold them to Hannah Oliver. In a weird twist the cobbler told police there was a scrap of packing paper in the sole of the shoes with the words 'commit no crime' on it. Anthony tried to conceal the shoes by hiding them in a haystack and then in his own home, but this 21-year-old was no master criminal and the shoes were found easily enough. When police prised the incriminating scrap of paper from the sole, there was no doubt left. The game was up, and Anthony Lingard was in trouble.

He was taken to Derby gaol to await his fate, and when it came, it wasn't a pretty one. Rebecca stood up in court and testified against her ex-lover and it took the judge a mere matter of minutes to reach a guilty verdict. Anthony Lingard was hanged at Derby on 28 March, but that wasn't the end of his punishment. From there soldiers carried his lifeless corpse back to Wardlow Mires where he was placed in a gibbet. His body was encased in the gibbet and hung on what was known by the macabre name of Gibbet Field, close to the scene of the crime. Anthony's body was left in the gibbet for months and reports of carnival crowds flocking to see the spectacle prompted some enterprising businessmen to set up stalls and booths around the attraction. Again, not everyone was happy about the practice or the way it was celebrated; the poet William Newton, on attending the scene, wrote of how horrified he was. Newton's writings, combined with complaints from the locals that Anthony's bones could be heard knocking at night as the gibbet swayed, keeping them from sleep, eventually forced the removal of Anthony.

Anthony Lingard was the last man to be gibbetted in Derbyshire, but it would be a few more years before the rest of the country followed suit and stopped hanging their criminals in this gruesome death chamber.

As a side note, Richard Felix who runs Derby gaol – the site of the last hanging, drawing and quartering in Britain and now a museum – at one time had what was reputed to be the skull of Anthony Lingard in his possession at the gaol. Although he has long since passed this artefact on, and he himself had his doubts about its authenticity, it's another startling example of how Lingard's story still persists today.

The Most Gruesome and Disturbing Story of the Potsford Gibbet

In 1699 not much was known about mental illness. The devil had a hold of you when you committed terrible acts, or else you were just plain evil. But it's doubtless that Jonah Snell had some sort of mental illness and suffered an 'episode' when he committed a shocking double murder in Suffolk. Jonah worked as servant to John Bullard who owned the water mill at Letheringham. It's not known what happened on this day in 1699, or why Jonah snapped in the way he did, but this was a blood thirsty attack and a sickening display that can only have been brought about by a troubled mind. Jonah attacked and killed John Bullard senior and his son John Bullard junior with an axe. The pair were found in the mill and had been 'hog-tied', a gruesome form of torture where their hands and feet were tied and their bodies hung upside down like slaughtered pigs from a beam. No one knows if the two men were treated in this way before they were killed, or if this was a bizarre post-mortem display. Jonah Snell did not attempt to avoid what he had done, if he was even completely aware of what he had done. He was found wandering around close by, his clothes covered in blood, the axe still in his hands. Confused, bewildered, and clearly in shock, this axe-wielding maniac was taken into custody where he offered no defence. We don't know why Jonah Snell committed this act, but there was only one punishment that would fit this crime – you could say it was the perfect punishment, because just as the Bullards had been hung up in a grisly display to be seen by others, so too was Jonah. He was hung at Potsford Wood. He reportedly had to be dragged on his back up to where the gallows stood, he was hanged and then hung in chains on the same spot, giving the name 'Dragarse' to the hill on which the gibbet stood. The gibbet post remains to this day and a plaque is attached to it reads: 'remains of Potsford Gibbet, in use at the end of seventeenth century, last known hanging April 14th 1699 Jonah Snell'. This was a single-use gibbet, as most were, and the terrible memory of what happened here is maintained.

And the 13th Hole at Chevin Golf Course

Sometime in the eighteenth century three men robbed the mail near the Chevin, Belper, in Derbyshire. There's little information remaining about this incident and the men's names are lost, but we do know that they were executed and then hung in chains, all three of them on the same gibbet. Sometime after this, the high gibbet post from which they all swung was set alight and the flames could be seen for miles. It's said that the tar which coated the bodies caused them to burn with such high flames, and that once this great fire had run its course only the gibbet irons were left. This is some of the most compelling evidence we have that we did tar bodies before they were gibbeted, something that is often talked of in reports from the time, but can't be easily proved. Today, at Chevin Golf Course, the 13th hole is affectionately named The Gibbet, as this is where the gruesome triple gibbet that burned down once stood.

Chapter 7

No Deterrent

A 2008 study by the university of Colorado found that 88 per cent of criminologists did not think the death penalty was a deterrent to crime. In 1993 the same study found 83 per cent felt the same way. So, as time moves on, it seems we realise more and more that the most extreme punishments do not stop anyone from committing a crime. We execute them, we have performed the most brutal forms of torture and post-mortem punishments on them, but still people commit murder.

On passing Spence Broughton's sentence, judge Justice Buller said 'That in order to deter others his punishment should not cease at the place of execution but his body should be suspended between earth and Heaven, as unworthy of either, to be buffeted by winds and storms.' But Spence Broughton would already have been aware of the gibbet as punishment for robbing the mail and the body of Frank Fearne was at that time still hanging in its iron cage on Loxley Moor in Sheffield, and neither of these things had deterred Spence Broughton.

William Burke of the famous body-snatching duo Burke and Hare was sentenced to death in 1829. At his sentencing the Lord Justice Clerk, David Boyle, stated that the only doubt in his mind was whether to satisfy the violated laws of the country and the voice of public indignation, meaning Burke's body ought to be exhibited in chains. However, in taking into consideration 'that the public eye would be offended by so dismal a spectacle', he stated that he was 'willing to accede to a more lenient execution of your sentence, and that your body should be publicly dissected.' He added that he hoped Burke's 'skeleton will be preserved in order that posterity may keep in remembrance your atrocious crimes.'

There's a lot to unravel here. William Burke had been busily both murdering people and robbing graves so he could sell the bodies on to surgeons for dissection. If we followed the 'eye for an eye' mentality, public dissection would perfectly fit the crime and would be poetic justice. But Lord Justice Boyle had considered hanging in chains for Burke because, a) it was written in law in the Murder Act that he could, and b) the public were outraged by Burke's crimes and so hanging in chains would show them justice very visibly. He seems to immediately contradict this by saying dissection would be better because the sight of his corpse swinging on the gibbet might offend people, and while the Murder Act does allow for gibbeting, it seems to prefer dissection. He ends by saying he hopes Burke's skeleton would be preserved as a reminder of the crimes; so, a deterrent? It seems ironic that the possibility of being caught, executed and dissected himself never stopped Burke from murdering others and ensuring they were dissected. William Burke's skeleton has indeed been preserved and is on display today at the Anatomical Museum at the University of Edinburgh. Unfortunately, it doesn't serve to remind us of how horrible his crimes were and teach us not to do bad things, rather it is a curiosity and something we can gaze at in wonder. It's unlikely Burke's dissection deterred anyone else from committing murder, the displaying of his skeleton certainly doesn't.

And what of hanging in chains? Did it work as a deterrent? Are there any known cases of the sight of gibbets putting anyone off committing a crime themselves? Apart from possibly the case of Thomas Harper, the answer is, no, not that we know of. There were celebrations of the gibbet and gibbeted men. There was certainly fear, but not fear that this might happen to us, only fear of the corpse and the ghosts we imagined these horrendous crimes and grotesque punishment produced. As a deterrent, it certainly didn't work. Crime did not go down during the time of gibbeting and the punishment seems to have often been viewed as a curiosity rather than something to make us think twice about committing similar crimes. Although we know in many cases it was a horrific thing to contemplate if you were the one being faced with this punishment, it does not appear to have stopped anyone from murdering, or from robbing the mail. In fact, there are instances of gibbets actually encouraging crimes.

In 1772 in Pewsey in Wiltshire William Amor murdered John Dyke. The pair had been drinking in the Swan Inn and it seems John Dyke had boasted a little too much about the amount of money he had on him. No doubt the drink had brought out his boastfulness and he flashed his cash around like a lord. On the way home that night William saw his opportunity and struck John Dyke over the head in order to steal his cash. Unfortunately, according to Amor, Dyke's death was an accident;

the blow proved fatal, but he never meant it to be. William protested he was innocent of murder as he had only meant to wound Dyke so he could take his money. This didn't wash and he was convicted of the murder and sentenced to death. William Amor was hung and then gibbeted on Pewsey Down on 16 March 1773. It was a famous case of the time and prompted many writings in newspapers and journals.

This from the *Bath Chronicle and Weekly Gazette*, 11 March 1773:

> On Friday last one William Amor, of Pewsey, in Hampshire, was committed to Fisherton Gaol, charged with the willful murder of John Dyke, Taylor, of Manningford Bruce, on the 23rd of November last [1772]. It seems his Wife and Family, wondering how the prisoner came by an unusual Quantity of money, spoke of it in Public, and several other circumstances concurring to throw a suspicion of his having committed the murder, he was taken up; when he confessed, that he waited under a hedge by the side of a Road, and when Mr. Dyke came by, he knocked him down with a large fold-stake; though he declared he meant only to rob him, and struck him that he might not recover his senses, so as to recollect who attacked him; but that he believes the first blow was the cause of his death. He directed them where to find the fold-stake; which was produced, very bloody, and tho' of an uncommon thickness, was broke towards the largest end in the struggle between the prisoner and the deceased.

And from the *Oxford Journal*, 27 March 1773:

> Last Tuesday Morning early, William Amor, capitally convicted at Salisbury Assizes, for the Murder of Mr. Dyke, of Manningford, was taken from Fisherton Gaol in a Post-Chaise, and carried to Pewsey-Down, where he was executed pursuant to his Sentence, and afterwards hanged in chains on the same gibbet.

As this was such a famous case, William's nephew Edward Amor certainly knew all about it. He may never have met his uncle, but fifty-two years after William was hanged in chains on Pewsey Down for assaulting and robbing John Dyke, Edward committed a very similar offence. So similar, we have to wonder at the apparent coincidence.

On Christmas Eve 1823 Edward Amor and John Goodman were drinking in Devizes when Thomas Alexander, perhaps the worst for wear, boasted of the profit he had made selling his wheat that day, a profit he carried on his person at that moment. Goodman and Amor followed Alexander that night when he left the inn and attacked him in order to steal his money. This time, however, the victim survived the attack and Thomas Alexander was able to testify. Strangely, although the pair were both convicted of the attack and sentenced to death, and both were pressured enormously to confess before they met their ends, neither of them buckled and both maintained their innocence until the end, Goodman even addressing the vast crowds at the gallows, said to be 20–30,000, and insisting upon his innocence. Perhaps because Goodman did this, or perhaps because of Amor's sullied name already, it was of general opinion that Goodman may indeed have been innocent, but no such grace was given to Edward Amor. When anyone did speak up for him they were promptly shot down, mostly with reference to his uncle, William Amor. The case and possible innocence of Goodman prompted many letters to be written to the press at the time. This letter published in the *Devizes Gazette* shows the strength of feeling around the case:

From the *Devizes and Wiltshire Gazette*, 6 May 1824:

> SIR – It is an error that all kinds of ministers visited Goodman and Amor; the clergymen alone of the parishes where they had lived or where they were confined, called on them with the Chaplain appointed by the Magistrates. Neither were they buoyed up by spiritual excitements to conceal, nor induced by any deceptions to confess their guilt. The truth indeed by all fair means was endeavoured to be elicited; and, at one time, it was asked Amor (on purpose to see if the similarity of the circumstances, with the awful horror attending thereon, would bring his own mind into a confidential confession of his offence), if it was true that his uncle had untimely suffered for a robbery and murder? – 'Yes Sir, (said he, with perfect calmness, and as answering a solemn question) so I have been told.' – 'You do not remember any thing of the affair?' 'Oh! No, Sir, it was long

before I was born. It was fifty-two years ago. My father was only a boy at plough.'

'Then you know nothing of that sad business?' 'I have often heard of it from others.' – (He seemed by no means disposed to conceal what he had heard, or to avoid talking upon the subject.) 'How did it happen?'

'They had been drinking at a public-house, Sir.' – 'Who?' 'My uncle and a tailor that lived at Shercott, named Dike.' 'Where were they drinking?' 'At the Swan, as it was called then, at Pewsey.'

'And what tempted your uncle to commit the deed?' 'The lust of money, Sir. The tailor, so they told me, had been boasting and showing his money at the Swan, and late at night sallied forth to go to Shercott; my uncle, who was very poor, soon afterwards went away, and followed him. He said his heart failed him once, and he turned back again; but there, he overtook him at last, and robbed and killed him.'

'Whereabout was it?' – 'Do you know the road, Sir, from Pewsey to Shercott?' – 'Very well, indeed, I have travelled it often.'

'It is about half-way; there are very plain marls now.' 'How marks?' – 'There are two great holes, just as you get over a stile.' 'What, the foot-way? I don't know the footway.'

'It is a very remarkable spot, Sir.'

'How was it discovered?' – 'His conscience, I have heard, was never at rest; and some suspected and watched him, and saw him throw the watch into a pond; and then he was taken up.'

A gentleman, who had not yet spoken, here slowly said to him, 'Did your uncle confess, Amor?' 'Oh! Yes, Sir; I have always heard there was no doubt of that, and he told himself, they say, all the particulars.'

This is related as near as possible, verbatim, and the manner in which Amor answered the questions, and narrated so trying a story, proved that he did not want understanding, or a conscientious sense of right and wrong; and he spoke with that firmness, which is equally removed from whining and canting, as from daringness and indifference. This conversation took place on the night before he suffered.

Sir, – Your correspondent, who said in your last week's Gazette that 'Amor's relations were dissenters, and disliked his going to church,' is misinformed.

Unfortunately for Amor, he was born of very ignorant parents, who paid no attention to the duties of religion, either as it regards their moral obligation to God, or their relative duties in bringing up their children in the fear of God. The elder branches of the Amor family were, and are remarkable for their ignorance of religion, and seldom or ever attend any place of religious worship, either church or chapel. They were never known regularly to attend a dissenting place of worship. I saw Amor, (accompanied by his wife,) at the chapel at Pewsey in September last; which, I believe, was the only time he was there. His father and mother I have seen there a few times during the past winter, which never occurred before. The grandfather of Amor was possessed of a small leasehold estate, and his grandmother was the mother of twenty children, nearly all of whom I knew, but none of them were or are dissenters. Your's,

JAMES NOYES.

Although Amor clearly knew all about his uncle's crime and punishment and didn't mind talking about it when asked, he doesn't seem to relate this to himself and his alleged crime at all. We can only assume he was either innocent, or he didn't see the two as connected. Mud sticks, and Amor would have been unfortunately tied to what his uncle had done. And as his family seem to come under criticism for the way they lived, Amor might have been in a situation where he didn't stand a chance. But with direct testimony from the victim himself, it's hard to see how this wasn't a case of history repeating itself.

Hannach Bocking

Just two years after Anthony Lingard became the last man to be gibbeted in Derbyshire another senseless murder would take place in the same village. In 1819 Hannah Bocking was 16 when she applied for a job as a maid servant. It's said she was turned down on account of her 'unamiable temper and disposition', perhaps a sign of things to come. Jane Grant, another local girl, unfortunately got the job ahead of Hannah, and Hannah was incensed. It was summertime in the village of Litten in Derbyshire and Hannah had a plan. She decided to become close friends with Jane and together one day they went to a field near Wardlow Mires for a picnic. It was a strange and macabre location for a picnic as the corpse of Anthony Lingard swung in its gibbet before them, a grisly reminder of what happened to those who murdered. Just why Hannah chose this location is hard to say, but she was by all accounts a strange girl with an ill temper and little feeling for others. It was here, with the two-year-old corpse of Lingard creaking in its chains, that Hannah offered Jane the spice cake she had made. This was a special cake that Hannah had made especially for the occasion and it contained one secret ingredient – arsenic. Hannah had purchased arsenic ten weeks earlier, telling the local surgeon from whom she had bought it that her grandfather needed to get rid of rats. Whether that was true or not, she used it for more than killing rats. After eating the spice cake Jane became very ill, suffering a great deal of pain. Before she died of the poisoning Jane was able to tell her parents about the cake and that she suspected this was what had made her so ill. Hannah was soon arrested and at first she implicated her sister, but eventually retracted this and took responsibility for the crime herself. Local reports at the time state that Hannah showed no emotion or remorse during her trial and that she was a depraved and wretched creature. On Monday 22 March 1819, just three years after Anthony Lingard was executed in front of Derby gaol, so too did Hannah Bocking meet her death for the crime of murder. Although still under the laws of the Murder Act, Hannah was not gibbeted following her execution, her body was taken from the gallows and sent for dissection. Anthony Lingard remained the last person to be hung in chains in this county.

But this story doesn't end there. In 1826 Anthony Lingard's younger brother William Lingard committed highway robbery within sight of the gibbet where Anthony's corpse, or what was left of it, still swung in its irons. The spectacle of his brother's body and the reminder of what he had done and what his punishment had been, did not deter William at all. Perhaps he even saw it as a badge of honour. Maybe, like so many criminal families, William was inspired by his older brother and entered into a life of crime to follow in his footsteps. Anthony Lingard's gibbet was purposely located high atop Peter's Stone so that everyone around could see it. But maybe this elevated position of Anthony's body had the opposite effect to that which was intended. By placing his gibbet so high on the hill, had the authorities given him something of an elevated status? Was he now a symbol for other would be criminals to look up to? If we think about the probability of gibbeting being an evolution of crucifixion, we can see how this may have worked. They were looking up to Anthony's body still hanging there, as followers of Jesus once looked up to his body on the cross. Did authorities create a martyr in Lingard instead of using him as a deterrent?

Highwaymen regularly encountered the gibbeted bodies of other thieves on the road, sometimes men they had known in life, and sometimes men they had worked the highways with. It never stopped any of them carrying on with their criminal lifestyles. The corpses of pirates were deliberately displayed at the Thames so other pirates could see them as they brought their ships to shore. They may have tipped their hats at their colleagues and said a prayer, but they did not give up piracy because of it.

And then there's the carnival that was often created around the gibbet. As Dickens remarked, the behaviour of the people attending the festivities around a gibbet was worse than the gibbet itself. This terrible punishment for terrible crimes seems to have brought out the worst in us. Pickpockets, prostitutes, drinkers and vandals, all attended and operated around the gibbet. Yes, they chose this place because this is where crowds congregated, but still, the sight of the criminal hanging dead and decaying in his chains did not stop any other criminals from carrying out their crimes. Instead, it became a means for them to do exactly that. Ironically, this was often the reason why gibbets were removed, as in Spence Broughton's case, and may have gone some way towards gibbeting being dispensed with altogether. But for the most part, because we placed so much importance on gibbets and their locations, they attracted yet more crime and unruly behaviour, instead of discouraging it.

Jerry Abershawe and The Bald Faced Stag

Location played a big part in the story of gibbeting. Locations for gibbets were considered and chosen for various reasons, though usually placed as close to the scene of the crime as possible. Was this done to tie the punishment to the crime? Was it done as a constant reminder of what had happened? As a deterrent? Whatever the reason behind it, the placing of gibbets had a massive impact on the landscape and those who lived in it, and on history and memory. When Jerry Abershawe, the bold highwayman, joined a gang in 1812 in his early criminal years, they chose The Bald Faced Stag in Finchley as their meeting place. The Bald Faced Stag Inn had already been standing since 1714 and had seen its share of characters and interesting occurrences by the time Jerry arrived. John Swan, perhaps the first man to be gibbeted following the Murder Act in 1752, had been known to collect his master from The Bald Faced Stag where he liked to drink. Perhaps John sometimes joined him there.

When John murdered his master, he was originally hung in chains in Epping Forrest, but later the gibbet was moved after some gentlemen complained of being able to see it from their homes. Swan was moved close to The Bald Faced Stag, seemingly on account of his and his victim's association with the pub. This is highly unusual and may have made the inn famous for a time as being the sight of a gibbet and of the chosen place for the victim to do his drinking. The pub tied together the murderer and the murdered in a way hardly ever seen before. It's doubtless that this fact was known when Jerry Abershawe and his gang decided to use the same inn as their headquarters years later. What better place to plan your crimes than at the scene of a famous crime, and in the long memory of what happened there? This was perhaps the perfect place for a criminal gang to meet. It had the nostalgia of a crime all around the building and as an inn, it provided the gang with somewhere to drink and be inconspicuous. Perhaps as in the case of Anthony Lingard's gibbet attracting further crime and serving as some sort of shrine, the inn was also seen by Abershawe and his gang as something to be proud of and footsteps to follow in.

The Bald Faced Stag still stands today and is an inn filled with history and memories. Today it is a smart and modern pub with no visible trace of the gibbet, but its walls have seen things we can only imagine.

Chapter 8

The Decline of the Gibbet

Rotted wooden posts, sometimes left standing for decades, re-enforced with metal supports to keep them upright for so long. The weight, as sunk into the slake, to give the entire structure its heavy ground anchor. Strong irons, made into body-shaped cages, but with hinges and screws so the cage could be fixed around the lifeless corpse and fastened there. These structures were built to last, and last they did; sometimes for scores of years. But what happened to the gibbets when they had served their purpose? What happened when these structures began to rot and rust?

The physical decline of gibbets varies. Gibbets were usually left standing until the weather dealt with them and they fell down, which could take decades. There are gibbet posts, like the Potsford gibbet, and irons, preserved and on display up and down the country. But most gibbets did not survive. In many cases the gibbets were dismantled because they had done their job, all that was left inside the cage was a skeleton, or sometimes just a skull, and it was time to remove them. When gibbets were taken down the bones were usually buried right there at the foot of the post. Sometimes skeletons were left in their irons and the whole thing was buried, and sometimes just the head irons containing the skull. Considering how many gibbets there were in our history, we have very few left preserved today. In many cases the posts were re-used, as fence posts, for gates, in barns and even as the beams in pubs. But when the time came for dismantling a gibbet, if it had been standing for decades, the wood and the irons would have been weather beaten and in bad shape. Some gibbets blew down in storms. Some were removed by new landowners who did not want this unsightly spectacle on their newly bought land. Some were tampered with by relatives and friends and either fell or were taken down in order to retrieve the remains of the criminal. But sometimes there is a story that illustrates how these structures became one with nature and how gibbeted men were not only at the mercy of the weather, but were also used by other creatures to continue life. Stephen Watson's gibbet is said to have become the home of a nest of starlings and in the book *Dunstaplelogia* by Charles Lamborn published 1859, it's reported that Gabriel Tomkins, a smuggler and highwayman, also had his skeleton used in this way and he made the perfect place for baby birds to be hatched, only this time the enterprising birds chose the man's skull to make their nest in.

> A man from Sewell, having robbed the mail coach upon the highway between Dunstable and Chalk Hill, was hung in chains at the corner of 'that close called Gib Close'. After the flesh and skins had wasted off and nothing remained but the bones, a pair of starlings built the nest in the skull and hatched their young. The brood was kept as pets by a local man. Lamborn does not give a date for this. The book also gives us an unusual example of a gibbet being destroyed, apparently for no good reason: 'The [gibbet] post was destroyed "by a party of wild Irish recruits" in 1803.'

But gibbets were not often vandalised completely. They were stolen from, pieces of the skeleton, the clothes, the gibbet itself, picked away at. They were tampered with. For the most part, they were dealt with by natural occurrences. Overwhelmingly, the weather took down the gibbet.

James Cully, Michael Quin, Thomas Quin and Thomas Markin were four Irishmen lodging at the William Marriott's farm at Wisbech in 1795. The four men murdered Mr Marriott one night and robbed the family of everything they had. In the attack, using a hatchet and pitchfork, the four also attempted to kill Mrs Marriott, but she survived and was able to give a full account of what had happened. The four men were caught and arrested, and sentenced to death. We can only assume that it was James Cully and Thomas Quin who dealt the vicious blows, as it was these two alone who were hung in chains after execution. Michael Quin and Thomas Markin were sent for dissection. Local constable John Peck wrote in his dairy that a great sea flood coming down the wash in 1831 had washed the gibbets away. Although we can't be certain that this was the case, after standing for thirty-six years the posts may have been easily felled by a torrent of seawater. John Peck's brother, Joseph Peck, managed to retrieve the prized head irons still containing a skull, and held them in his private collection at Bevis Hall. It was never known if the irons and skull belonged to Cully or

Quin. The head irons, known as 'Paddy's night cap' are now on display at the Wisbech and Fenland Museum, along with John Peck's diary.

Gibbet posts would have been rotten in many cases by the time they were removed, and some posts that were found and preserved later on, like the Scrooby post once stored at Doncaster Museum and Spence Broughton's post which was unearthed and displayed in the yard of a nearby pub, have long since disappeared. When the gibbet of William Suffolk was dismantled in North Walsham, Norfolk, following his gibbeting in 1797 for the murder of Mary Beck, it's said the post was preserved at Royston House (no longer standing) and was later gifted to a museum.

William had been courting Mary, much to the disapproval of Mary's brother who wanted William to stay away from his sister. After the pair had argued over this William told Mary's brother he'd show him 'a great alteration; that night'. But William had no intention of leaving Mary alone, instead when he met her later that evening he beat her to near death with a stick. Mary was able to name him as her attacker before she died and on hearing this the *Gentleman's Magazine* records his reply as 'if he had thought she could have stirred hand or foot he would have beaten her till this time'. Sadly we don't have any records to suggest which museum this post was given to or what happened to the post. There is no trace of it now. We have to presume these hunks of wood either rotted and were no longer in good enough condition to be thought of as being worth anything or useful, or they were mistaken for nothing but dead old wood and thrown out. What happened to the many gibbet cages is more of a tantalising mystery. Irons were sturdy and built to last and though we can see from some gibbet irons today, like Ralph Smith's head irons in the Boston Guildhall Museum, that there is some rust and decay, they would remain intact if kept and stored. It's said Frank Fearne's gibbet blew down in a storm at Christmas time, but we have no record of what happened to his gibbet or where it went. Many irons have been lost, buried with the bones and never recovered, or unearthed years later and either used for other purposes or passed into private hands and forgotten and disappeared. Who knows how many sets of irons are still underground yet to be discovered?

The physical decline of the gibbets themselves is one of nature and circumstance. Wood rots and is easy to saw through or set alight. Screws can be filed and undone, allowing an iron cage to fall or be taken down. Bones and entire structures can be buried and given to the land. But the social decline of gibbets and gibbeting had to be led by a few forward thinking people, and the rest of us had to be persuaded.

If we go right back to the beginning of the story of gibbeting, or at least as far back as reliable history allows us, we can find some odd reasoning as to why we did this in the first place. As laws changed and wording altered some things slipped through the net and some things were confused. It appears to have been a Roman law that stipulated bodies be left in their gibbet irons and on display, and this comes with some unexpected reasoning 'so that they may be deterred and the conspictus others, it is a comfort to me, and his kinsmen of the slain.'

Albert Hartshorne confirms this when he tells us in his book *Hanging In Chains* that one of the reasons behind the use of the gibbet was to give comfort to the family of the victim. It's hard to see how the sight of the murderer's corpse hanging for decades and rotting before their eyes could have been a comfort, and we know in some cases it certainly wasn't because it was the families of the victims who asked for the gibbet to be moved, so much anguish did it cause them. But it is perhaps easy to see how it worked as revenge. If we look back over the story of hanging in chains it does seem to have been largely driven by society's need for visible justice, or at lease society's perceived need for this visual display of rightful punishment. Once the criminal had been executed his body legally belonged to the state and they could do with it what they saw fit, but when it comes to gibbeting it often had more to do with what the community wanted rather than what the state thought was right and just. Gibbeting was done to appease the people and for the appearance of delivering justice. It wasn't to give comfort to the victims and their families, it was to keep the peace.

Gibbeting was a rare occurrence, something which made it all the more shocking when it was performed. If we take the county of Lincolnshire in the years between 1736 and 1798, covering the era both immediately before and after the introduction of the Murder Act, we can see there are only four recorded cases of hanging in chains, and all for murder.

William Tyler, Murder, March 1742
Hanged at Spalding and afterwards in chains at Pinchbeck
   Drainside

Thomas Brown, Murder, 28 March 1759
Hanged in chains at Ancholm Corner near Spital

Philip Heaton (Hooton), Murder of Samuel Stockton,
    6 March 1769
Hanged in chains on Surfleet Common

Ralph Smith, Murder of Gentle Sutton, 16 March 1792
Hanged in chains at Frampton

In addition to this there is one entry that simply states execution by hanging, again for murder.

Daniel Ryan, Murder of John Butterton, August 1762
Hanged on Lincoln City gallows.

There are eleven other murders which carried a sentence of execution, presumably hanging though it isn't stated, and no mention of hanging in chains. One of these carried the punishment of burning at the stake for a female murderer. There are seventeen cases of highway robbery, all carrying the sentence of death, seven cases of burglary, fourteen cases of horse theft, eleven cases of housebreaking, fourteen cases of stealing livestock, two cases of arson, and one case of sodomy or bestiality. All carrying the sentence of death.

Although the range of crimes for which people were sentenced to death is shocking, it does illustrate how rare gibbeting was. It's hard to say why twelve of the murders committed over this period aren't stated as carrying the further post-mortem punishment of hanging in chains. Some cases of hanging in chains are clearly due to particularly brutal murders (though not always), and those bodies that were not gibbeted would have been sent for dissection. It could have been because of cost, or it could have been a line being drawn between murder and barbarous murder. Gibbeting was, after all, carried out at the discretion of judging authorities. Most surprising of all is that none of the seventeen recorded cases of highway robbery, not a single one, appears to have resulted in hanging in chains, perhaps leading us to surmise this practice carried out on highwayman was much rarer than we tend to believe.

By the early nineteenth century opinion was on the turn, and although the general public still enjoyed a good old hanging and attendance at hangings and gibbetings was still high, the authorities and intellectuals of the time had begun to seriously question the practice. Apart from the gruesome nature not being fitting for a civilised society like our own, scientists and medical professionals began to determine the link between rotting corpses and filth in general, and sickness and disease. When the Brontë sisters were in their twenties and living in Haworth in Yorkshire the average life expectancy for women in the village was just 25. Factors like death in childbirth came into play, but it was also discovered that because open sewage ran down the street, including excrement, there was a higher chance of serious illness. Worse than that, decomposing matter from the graveyard at the top of the hill was found to have seeped into the water supply and was causing rampant disease, especially among the women, who were most likely to be in their homes during the day.

As we learned more about disease and filth in our environment, we began to see the gibbet as something putrid, but we also began to understand the need for more humane punishments, even within the death sentence. This was what separated us from the murderers; we had compassion. Perhaps, instead of looking at the gibbet and it reinforcing in us our distance from these men and their crimes, we began to see the gibbet as something that made us almost as bad as they were. Perhaps. It would take some time before people en masse saw the situation that way. But opinions were changing fast and so was our taste for torture and capital punishment.

As noted, the Anatomy Act of 1832 made some important changes to how we dealt with murderers. Dissection by surgeons was a big problem prior to the Act because the demand for cadavers far outstripped supply, leading to some pretty horrendous criminal activities, such as the famous case of Burke and Hare. Because the Murder Act stated that only murderers were to be dissected (or hung in chains), surgeons eager to get their hands on corpses for research were having to wait a long while. There just weren't that many murderers. The Anatomy Act of 1832 states that instead of murderers, dissection could be performed on any unclaimed body. This usually meant the poor, people who had died in hospital alone, or in the workhouse. There was considerable objection to this as the implication was that if you died poor your body was fair game for surgeons to do with what they liked, but if you were rich there would be no such horrors performed on you.

They tell us it was necessary for the purposes of science. Science? Why, who is science for? Not for poor people. Then if it be necessary for the purposes of science, let them have the bodies of the rich, for whose benefit science is cultivated.

William Cobbett

The Anatomy Act also stated that murderers were now to be either buried within the prison walls or to be hung in chains, instead of being publicly dissected. Public dissection was out, but publicly hanging in chains was still ok. This was an interesting move. The insistence that murderers were not to be given a burial had gone, and there was now a much wider moral gap between how we treated them. They were to be given either a burial in the prison grounds with an unmarked grave, or a grave bearing only their initials, or they were to be encased in that body shaped iron cage and left on the gibbet as they always had been. An unmarked grave within the prison walls still wasn't a Christian burial in a churchyard, but it was a burial. Faced with either that or the traditional gibbeting, criminals must have wondered at the workings of modern post-mortem treatments.

The Anatomy Act solved the problem of bodies needed for medical research, as we had far more paupers going spare than we had murderers, but it wasn't a popular act for many reasons. It put less importance on the bodies of the poor than on the rich, many people in all areas of society were against dissection entirely, and it also continued the practice of hanging in chains for murderers. Though this wouldn't last much longer.

The Last Man to be Gibbeted in Britain

In August of 1832 James Cook became the last man to be gibbeted in Britain. James Cook was a bookbinder in Leicester and it seems that the expenses incurred in the trade of bookbinding were more than he could afford. James Cook was in considerable debt to Mr Paas, a London maker of brass instruments that Cook needed for his bookbinding. When Mr Paas came to Leicester to collect on his debt, James Cook couldn't pay and instead he murdered Mr Paas and tried to conceal what he had done. He might have got away with it; Cook was said to be of good

131

character and nobody would have thought he could murder a man, but Cook needed a way to dispose of the body and this would be his downfall.

He decided to burn the body in the grate of his workshop. At first no one thought anything of this, it was a workshop and sometimes there was a fire burning in there, but on this particular evening the flames inside the workshop were so great Cook's neighbours thought the building was burning down and rushed in to try and put out the fire. On entering the workshop, Cook's neighbours discovered a piece of flesh on top of the fire. Cook said it was horse meat, but something didn't seem right and, sure enough, further investigation uncovered the charred bones and remains of a man. James Cook confessed to the murder of Mr Paas and that he had cut the body into pieces and burned the whole of him. The way in which Cook had attempted to dispose of the body is the part of this murder that shocked people, and it was this that made the judge impose the, by then very rare, further punishment of hanging in chains. In this case, considering Cook's previous good character and standing in the community, hanging him in chains wasn't only justice, and it wasn't just revenge. The act of stringing him up like that for everyone to stare at also brought shame on him. He might have been dead by this time, but he was still being shamed for what he had done.

From the Newgate Calendar:

> When the body of the convict had hung the usual time after his execution, it was cut down and conveyed back to the jail, in order that the necessary preparations might be made to carry out that portion of the sentence which directed his remains to be gibbeted in chains. The head was shaved and tarred, to preserve it from the action of the weather; and the cap in which he had suffered, was drawn over his face. On Saturday afternoon his body, attired as at the time of his execution, having been firmly fixed in the irons necessary to keep the limbs together, was carried to the place of its intended suspension in Saffron-lane, not far from the Aylestone Toll-gate, a short distance out of the town of Leicester. A gallows, thirty-three feet in height, had been already erected; and the horrible burden which it was intended to bear was soon attached to it. On the following day, thousands of persons were attracted to

the spot, to view this novel but most barbarous exhibition; and considerable annoyance was felt by persons residing in the neighbourhood of the dreadful scene. Representations were, in consequence, made to the authorities, and on the following Tuesday morning, instructions were received from the Home Office, directing the removal of the gibbet, and granting the remission of that portion of the sentence, by which this exposure, the remnant only of a barbarous age, was required. These orders were immediately obeyed; and the body was subsequently buried in Leicester.

Vast crowds had attended Cook's public execution and also his gibbeting. The public in general still loved their hangings and still wanted to stand and stare at this most remarkable sight when a murderer was hung in chains. But this was to be the very last time. Unlike most other gibbetings, James Cook's body only hung in chains for a matter of days. The complaints about the smell, the sight, and the atmosphere of the gibbet were enough to ensure it was removed swiftly. Although an estimated 40,000 people attended this spectacle, those who had to live near to it did not approve. It was the crowds themselves that offended some residents, while for others having to look at this gruesome form of post-mortem punishment was too much. Gibbeting was no longer thought of as an appropriate way to bring justice and in parliament moves were being made to abolish it altogether.

William Ewart was a liberal politician, often called an 'abolitionist' due to his tireless work to end extreme punishments, torture, senseless executions, and slavery. In 1832 he introduced a Bill to end capital punishment for stealing sheep, cattle, and horses, something which was once a sign of how important and valuable these animals were to us, but which no longer made any sense. He recognised how much the world was changing and how much our laws needed to change with it. In 1834 he introduced a Bill to abolish hanging in chains.

From the Commons Sitting, Parliament:

HC Deb 13 March 1834 vol 22 cc155-7 155
Mr. Ewart moved for leave to bring in a Bill to take away from Judges the power of directing criminals, in certain cases, to be hanged in chains. From what had fallen from

the right hon. Secretary for Ireland, on a former evening, he believed, if he had understood the right hon. Member rightly, that Government would be willing to abolish this odious practice of hanging murderers in chains. It was unnecessary for him, therefore, to enter into the question, and he should only submit his Motion, to the judgment of the House.

When William Ewart introduced the Bill to parliament to abolish hanging in chains completely, he and the Bill faced no opposition. This now outdated and most gruesome post-mortem punishment had finally had its time. When the Bill went through the House of Lords, Lord Suffield remarked that he could see no reason to continue with such an odious practice. There were no amendments made to the Bill and it went through the day after its third reading with no debate. Hanging criminals in chains was over.

What's most incredible about this is that it took until 1834 to officially abolish the weird and macabre practice of gibbeting. But there was still work to do when it came to how we treated criminals and prisoners, how we dealt with crimes and criminals, and how we punished them.

Following Charles Dickens's attendance at the public hanging that appalled him so much, he appealed to the public to recognise the barbarity of their behaviour and of the acceptance of this public form of punishment and entertainment.

From his letter to *The Times*, 1849:

> I wish to turn this dreadful experience to some account for the general good, by taking the readiest and most public means of adverting to an intimation given by Sir G. Grey in the last session of Parliament, that the Government might be induced to give its support to a measure making the infliction of capital punishment a private solemnity within the prison walls (with such guarantees for the last sentence of the law being inexorably and surely administered as should be satisfactory to the public at large), and of most earnestly beseeching Sir G. Grey, as a solemn duty which he owes to society, and a responsibility which he cannot for ever put away, to originate such a legislative change himself ...

I have seen, habitually, some of the worst sources of general contamination and corruption in this country, and I think there are not many phases of London life that could surprise me. I am solemnly convinced that nothing that ingenuity could devise to be done in this city, in the same compass of time, could work such ruin as one public execution, and I stand astounded and appalled by the wickedness it exhibits. I do not believe that any community can prosper where such a scene of horror and demoralization as was enacted this morning outside Horsemonger Lane Gaol is presented at the very doors of good citizens, and is passed by, unknown or forgotten. And when in our prayers and thanksgivings for the season we are humbly expressing before God our desire to remove the moral evils of the land, I would ask your readers to consider whether it is not a time to think of this one, and to root it out.

William Marwood was a cobbler turned hangman, working for the British government at Lincoln Castle between 1872 and 1883. When Marwood first started working at Lincoln Castle executions were public. Today you can stand in 'Cobb Hall', a small tower at the corner of the walls of the castle where a gallows was erected and prisoners were hung. Crowds would gather outside the castle walls and watch the spectacle from the ground, the prisoner hoisted high above them. This is where Ralph Smith, John Keale, and Tom Otter were most likely executed before being fitted into their irons and taken back to the scenes of their crimes to be gibbeted. Inside the castle walls today the door to Cobb Hall remains closed. Inside this dingy dark space is where the prisoners would wait for their execution. Although this isn't open to the public, it's said that the walls inside the tower are covered in the scratches of the desperate men, their death by the slow strangulation of hanging via the short drop looming in front of them. When public execution was abolished in 1868 it meant prisoners were alone with their hangman when they suffered their fate. Marwood and many of his fellow hangmen found this distressing, as hanging by the traditional short drop was a long drawn out process that saw prisoners die an excruciating death.

The withdrawal of the crowds from this brutal form of execution changed the entire experience. Hanging was no longer something that was celebrated and used as a dark form of entertainment, or as a reassurance to the public that justice was being done. With the crowds eliminated, hanging was now an intimate and very intense experience shared only by the prisoner and the hangman. Now it was up close and personal, the prisoner a fellow human being from which you are about to extinguish life, and in a most painful and slow process; it can't have been an easy thing to go through. The crowds had served as a kind of buffer for the brutality of hanging by the short drop. There's safety in numbers, and once that was gone, hangmen were faced with the nightmares of what they were doing. So, in 1872 Marwood persuaded the governor of Lincoln Castle to let him perform an experiment. The 'long drop' that Marwood invented at Lincoln Castle allowed for the neck of the prisoner to break instantly, giving them a swift and relatively painless death. Executions moved from the viewing tower of Cobb Hall to the larger more private Lucy's Tower. On the ground before you walk up the steps to Lucy's Tower today the small, pet-like graves of hanged men and women are scattered around the ground like rocks in a river. They have nothing more marking them than the initials of the dead. These graves are stepping stones in our progress from brutal torture and extreme forms of execution and post-mortem punishments, to the recognition of criminals as troubled and broken human beings and our place in bringing humane justice to a civilised society.

We may have witnessed the decline of gibbets themselves and the decline of gibbeting in society, but we still held onto the collective memory of what had happened for many years after, in songs, plays, books, and in landmarks and roads that bore the name of those gibbeted or the gibbet itself. It is now almost 200 years since we abolished gibbeting and in that time we, as a society, have largely forgotten about this terrible post-mortem punishment. Where there are still reminders in the landscape most of us don't realise what they refer to. In the case of buildings being named after gibbetings, such as farms, cottages, and inns, many of these are lost as some buildings are demolished and ownership of buildings change.

Thomas Busby murdered his father-in-law, Daniel Auty, in 1702 in Thirsk, Yorkshire. Neither Thomas nor Daniel were gentlemen; Daniel was a known counterfeiter and Thomas was a drunk and a vile-tempered thug. Daniel Auty may have had his faults and been a criminal himself, but he couldn't stand by and watch his own daughter put up with the terrible treatment handed out by Busby. One night, Daniel Auty waited for Thomas to arrive at his local pub, as he always did. Daniel was out to show Thomas who was boss and he sat in Thomas's favourite chair in the pub while he waited. The sight of the father-in-law he already hated sitting in his chair in his pub, drove Thomas Busby to red hot anger. The pair argued and later that night Thomas arrived at Daniel's house and beat him to death with a hammer. Busby was caught and sentenced to death. Following his execution he was hung in chains at the crossroads outside the pub.

The poet William Grainge wrote in 1859:

> The bones of the poor wretch who had committed murder were hung to fester in the sunshine and blow in the tempest until they fell piecemeal to earth and tradition yet tells tales of night wanderers being terrified when passing this dreaded spot.

Following this terrible murder and lasting punishment the pub was renamed 'The Busby Stoop Inn' because of the 'stoop', or post, still being in place outside the pub long after the irons and the corpse had been removed. As the years went by the pub gained a reputation as being haunted and what was said to be the famous chair at the centre of Thomas and Daniel's argument that night still waited in the pub for brave drinkers to sit in. The chair was supposedly cursed and reports ran wild of people sitting in it then dying later. The chair was eventually given to Thirsk Museum by a landlord who was afraid of the curse killing his customers. The chair hangs from a ceiling today, so that no one can sit in it, just to be on the safe side. And the pub? Although the Busby Stoop Inn hung onto the story of the gibbet for many years, hanging a mock-up noose from its exterior once the original post was gone, and keeping the memory of Thomas Busby and what had happened here alive, it has finally let go of this dark and troubled memory. The Busby Stoop is now Jaipur Spice. The pub became an Indian restaurant in 2013 after its former passing trade and interested ghost hunters died down. The gibbet post and replica noose are long gone, and the cursed chair is in the museum. The building itself remains, but it is the loss of these physical reminders that allow the reality of the gibbet to fade from our collective memory.

But some reminders of crimes and punishments are more lasting. At Nottingham's Museum of Crime and Justice you can walk in the exercise yard where prisoners spent many hours pacing and wandering. On the outside wall of what was their gaol is prisoner graffiti. The scratches on the wall here are not desperate like those inside the cell at Cobb Hall. These are thoughtful and have more of a 'I was here' feel about them. In some cases they were simply the prisoner's chance to record the facts of when and why he was there. On pale sandstone the words 'S Clark condemned at March 10 for house breaking at Sutton in Ashfield', are bold and plain to see. In other places the word 'hell' is carved and sometimes initials and a date like 'I.M 1896'. The prisoners here had time on their hands and not much to do with it, and so they recorded who they were, when and why they were there, and how they felt about it. They set their memories in stone for us to see today.

Times have changed greatly and our brutal forms of torture, executions, and post-mortem punishments are in our past. This is our history. Along with other macabre practices like hanging, drawing, and quartering, hanging in chains is a curiosity to us now. It's something we still stare at in wonder and fascination, even though the irons no longer contain corpses and all that remains in some cases is a street name, a plaque, or the memory of what happened in verse and song.

Chapter 9

A Modern Fascination

In William Andrew's book *Bygone Punishments* published in 1899, he writes: 'THE time is not so far distant when the gibbet and gallows were common objects in this country'. The fascination with this extraordinary form of post-mortem punishment was high enough to warrant a whole chapter in this book, a mere sixty years after the practice had been abolished. Our fascination with the displaying of the bodies of criminals, especially murderers, is nothing new. When Robert Carlton murdered Mary Frost in 1741 in Diss, Norfolk, the whole town became voyeurs and were highly excited by what had happened. Carlton was known to be guilty of the crime of sodomy, though as he was an excellent tailor and by all accounts a quiet man who kept himself to himself, the people in his community never sought to have him prosecuted. At that time, of course, Carlton was running the risk of arrest and imprisonment, even the death penalty, simply for being gay. But everyone in Diss liked him so he was left to himself. It was when Carlton met John Lincoln that things changed. Lincoln became Carlton's lodger and the pair soon became lovers. Carlton never tried to keep his affections for Lincoln a secret and the whole town knew what was going on. Maybe because of the infamy, or perhaps simply because he got bored of Carlton, Lincoln soon started to wander and it wasn't long before he met the pretty Mary Frost and decided he would leave his former life with Carlton and marry her.

It seems likely the pair argued bitterly over this decision because, in a cruel act of defiance, Lincoln brought Mary to the house to meet Carlton. Carlton was not amused and threatened to throw her out on the street and also suggested that if she was ever brought to the house again he would do her harm. But she was brought to the house again, and this time at Carlton's own invitation. Carlton invited Mary over for tea and then proceeded to coldly poison her. Because the whole town knew how Carlton and Lincoln lived and the particulars of the affair, Carlton was soon arrested and tried for murder and sodomy. He was found guilty and sentenced to death and then hanging in chains. But there was a further interlude of morbid fascination for the people of Diss when, following his execution, Carlton's lifeless body was taken back to the house where the murder had been committed. He was strung up in the middle of the room and anyone who wanted to inspect him for signs of his evil, or just gawk at this murderer's body, could pay two pence for entry. The viewing went down a storm and when the crowds had all taken their turn at staring at the corpse, Carlton's body was ceremoniously hung up in his gibbet irons for further viewing.

Extract of a Letter from DISS, dated 8 April 8 1742:

> Last Saturday Robert Carlton (who was condemn'd at the last Thetford Assizes for Sodomy, and the Murder of a young Woman by Poison) was brought hither from Norwich Castle. Sunday in the Afternoon he was carried to Church, where an excellent Sermon, applicable to the Criminal's Condition, was preached before the largest Congregation ever seen here. The next Day he was executed upon our Common, and afterwards hanged in Chains. He behaved to the last with very little shew of Remorse; and altho' he acknowledged the Sodomy, yet, when the Rope was about his Neck at the Gallows, he denied that he was guilty of the Murder. The People present at the Execution were computed by some at 15,000, and by others at 20,000. (*Ipswich Journal*)

We might reassure ourselves that we are better than the people of Diss and we don't do anything as dark as this today, but how many of us would have joined that queue for the chance to inspect the body of our town's most famous and terrible murderer?

Today we are still intrigued by murder and our own history of execution and post-mortem punishments. There are fifteen museums in Britain with gibbet irons in their collections and nothing pulls a crowd quite like a special exhibition of gruesome artefacts.

In 2011 Sheffield Museums hosted an exhibition called Sheffield's Horrible History. Among the exhibits was a prisoner's belt and shackles, thought to have been the irons Spence Broughton was transported to and from prison in.

The National Crime and Justice Museum in Nottingham offers a tour of the former cells of the gaol, and on display is a full-body gibbet cage, thought to be James Cook's, the last man to be gibbeted in Britain, along with stocks and a ducking stool. There's even a mock up gallows complete with hangman's noose.

In Lincoln Castle you can tour the Victorian cells, a marked improvement on the earlier cells at Nottingham, but still incredibly small and dark. You can walk in Cobb Hall and Lucy's Tower where hangings took place and you can weave in and out of the small stumps of prisoners' graves in the grounds.

At The Boston Guildhall Museum a tiny mediaeval courtroom blooms around an equally tiny spiral staircase that leads down to the cells of the condemned men below. Ralph Smith's head irons are kept at the museum, along with the tobacco box made from his gibbet and the calling card of hangman William Marwood, the inventor of the long drop.

In January 2018 North Lincolnshire Museum kicked off a year-long display, named Cruel Beauty. The exhibition showcased the regions historical objects associated with crime and punishment, that are at the same time macabre and beautiful in their craftmanship and artistry. The display included the nutcrackers made from Tom Otter's gibbet irons.

Other museums containing gibbets across the country are:

Louth Museum – John Keale's gibbet cage
Rye Castle Museum – John Bread's gibbet cage
Doddington Hall – Tom Otter's head-irons
South Shield's Museum – Willian Jobbling's gibbet cage
Museum of Docklands – a pirate's gibbet cage
Warrington Museum – Edward Miles's gibbet irons
Winchester Westgate Museum – Jack the Painter's gibbet irons
Norwich Castle – Stephen Watson's gibbet irons
The Norris Museum, Cambridgeshire – Gervase Matcham's gibbet iron belt
Reading Museum – Tull or Hawkin's leg-iron
Moyse Hall Museum – John Nichols's gibbet cage
Wisbech and Fenland Museum – Thomas Quinn or James Culley's head-irons.
St Fagans Museum – Sion y Gof's head-irons
Haslemere Museum – part of the gibbet post three men were hung in chains from for the murder of an unknown sailor. A highly unusual triple gibbet.

The lure of the ghost story is still a hard one to ignore and most of these relics and locations of gibbets have some supernatural stories attached to them. John Nichols's gibbet cage hangs from the ceiling at Moyse Hall Museum and is said to be haunted. John Nichols was executed along with his 19-year-old son Nathanial in 1794 for the murder of their daughter/sister, Sarah. Whoever dealt the blows beat her to death with a hedge stake and then strangled her for good measure. No one knows why Sarah was killed and the two Nichols men went to the gallows protesting their innocence and each accusing the other. Nathaniel was then sent for dissection and John was hung in chains at the scene of the crime at Honington. Perhaps it was presumed the elder man, then 59, was more likely to have committed this very brutal attack, even if they were both implicated and participated in the murder, and so it was he alone who was hung in chains. Neither of them ever confessed it. In 1938 at what was then Honington aerodrome, the gibbet was discovered, with the entire skeleton of John Nichols still in the cage, still wearing his boots. It may have been this fact that really got the ghost hunters excited and the locals fearful. A complete skeleton within a gibbet cage was a rare enough find, but with his boots still on, that was unheard of. This gibbet cage, surely, had to be haunted. Many visitors, and even staff members at the museum, talk of that eerie feeling of not being alone.

In 1787 three sailors, James Marshall, Michael Casey and Edward Lonegon, killed another sailor near Hindhead. The unfortunate sailor had been kind enough to pay for the other three's drinks that evening as they went from pub to pub on their way back to their ship at Portsmouth. Sadly, this generosity only fuelled the three men's greed and they took their opportunity in a quiet spot to rob and kill him.

The Hampshire Chronicle 2 October 1786:

> Sunday last a shocking murder was committed by three sailors, on one of their companions, a seaman also, between Godalming — They nearly severed his head from his body, stripped him quite naked, and threw him into a valley, where he was providentially discovered, soon after the perpetration of the horrid crime, by some countrymen corning over Hind Head, who immediately gave the alarm, when the desperadoes were instantly pursued, and overtaken at the house of Mr. Adams, the Sun, at Rake. They were

properly secured, and are since lodged in gaol, to take their trials at the next assizes for the county of Surrey.

The name of the murdered sailor is lost, but the gibbet post from which the three were hung survives and is on display at Haslemere Museum. The sailor who was murdered is buried in Thursley churchyard. Following this incident and the gibbeting, the hill was named Gibbet Hill and it soon became known for being haunted. James Stillwell erected a memorial stone at the sight of the crime. The inscription on the stone reads:

ERECTED
In detestation of a barbarous Murder
Committed here on an unknown Sailor
On Sep, 24th 1786
By Edwd. Lonegon, Mich. Casey & Jas. Marshall
Who were all taken the same day
And hung in Chains near this place
Whoso sheddeth Man's Blood by Man shall his
Blood be shed. Gen Chap 9 Ver 6

It seems the stone was erected very soon after the event. The three men were gibbeted here in September 1786 and the stone was supposedly also placed here that same year. An inscription on the back of the stone reads:

THIS STONE
was Erected
by order and at
the cost of
James Stilwell Esqr.
of
Cosford
1786
Cursed be the Man who injureth
or removeth this Stone

We can't be sure this was the case, but if it was, then the gibbeted men would surely still have been hanging here at the time too, meaning the stone was erected in the long shadow of the three murderers swinging from their gibbets. The inscription on the back, with the warning of a curse if the stone was moved, was added after the stone had in fact been moved. In 1826 it was taken from where it stood and placed alongside the 'punch bowl bend', the busy road that skirts the edge of the Punchbowl crater, due to the road at the original site being realigned. When it was returned back to its original location the warning was added to the back of the stone. We can speculate about why this was done, but the fear surrounding gibbet sites, and the threat of ghosts and curses was keenly felt. In Charles Dickens's novel *Nicholas Nickleby*, published 1839, a scene describes the terrible spectre of this murder and how much the gibbet was still casting fear and unease among anyone who passed by the area, especially near the Devil's Punchbowl. This 282 hectare depression in the land has many legends and tales associated with it and is called such as it was said to have been made when the devil scooped out the land in anger:

> They walked upon the rim of the Devil's Punch Bowl; and Smike listened with greedy interest as Nicholas read the inscription upon the stone which, reared upon that wild spot, tells of a murder committed there by night. The grass on which they stood, had once been dyed with gore; and the blood of the murdered man had run down, drop by drop, into the hollow which gives the place its name. 'The Devil's Bowl,' thought Nicholas, as he looked into the void, 'never held fitter liquor than that!

In 1851 the Whig politician William Erle paid for a Celtic cross to be erected on Gibbet Hill, at the exact spot on which the gibbet post had stood. Local people were so afraid to go near the hill and were so terrified of the ghosts of the three murderers, William decided a holy monument was the only way to put their minds at rest. The Latin inscription on the cross translates as 'Light after darkness. Peace in passing away. Hope in light. Salvation after death'. As it was placed where the three murderers were gibbeted it seems to be suggesting they are the ones to receive peace, light and hope, the very opposite of what the gibbet had attempted to achieve. Although we don't know what became of the remains of the three men or their irons, we do have part of the gibbet post. In 2017 an episode of the BBC's *Flog It!* centred on the story and the relic at Haslemere Museum. As the presenter spoke of this terrible murder and the following events, fears, hauntings, and moves to bring calm to the area, he held up the preserved part of the post at the very spot where it had originally stood, reuniting it with its first location and the place it had been used to suspend three corpses.

Our relationship with the gibbet is a curious one and swings from fascination, dark humour, and the belief in its power to cure and heal us; to fear, unease and the belief that it is haunted by evil. Combe Gibbet, that famous landmark that saw perhaps the only woman known to have been gibbeted in Britain, is today the central focus of organised walks. The AA sets out a 7 mile walk on its website that takes in The Swan Inn, the seventeenth-century pub that was standing at the time of the shocking events at Inkpen, and passes the Crown and Garter Inn, the very pub where the bodies of the two murderers were taken following their execution. The walk culminates in the site of the imposing double gibbet on the hill. Combe Gibbet is so important as a piece of history and as social commentary, it has been replaced every time it has been destroyed, seven times so far. It's not known how long the original gibbet actually stood for, but we know the first post, erected in 1676 had rotted so badly it was replaced in 1850. This post was struck by lightening and was replaced again in 1949. There is no record of what happened to this third post, but it stood for only one year and was replaced again in 1950. There was some ceremony around the erecting of this fourth gibbet. Newspaper reports tell of a 50ft, 150-year-old oak tree being made into a 30ft post, paid for by public subscription and erected to perpetuate the grim justice carried out at that place. Over 1,000 people watched the spectacle and BBC cameras attended to record the event.

Not everyone saw this landmark and the meaning behind it as something to celebrate however. In 1965 and again in October 1969 the post was sawn down by protesters against hanging. An ironic twist of fate for the Combe Gibbet, so celebrated for bringing justice via the lasting punishment of hanging in chains. Still, this most remarkable gibbet post persisted. Although local newspapers in 1969 reported that there was little enthusiasm among the community for replacing the post, on 4 June 1970 a new one was erected.

On 18 June 1970, in the run-up to the general election, an effigy was hung from the gibbet with political slogans strewn around it. Labour MP Tim Simms saw the opportunity to make something of this and laid flowers at the gibbet in memory of the injustices to the common people by a cruel feudal system, which we as a society had brought to an end through compassion. Mr Simms drew parallels between this and the constant battle for equality in our society. Eight years later this post blew down in strong winds. In 1979 the gibbet was re-erected for the sixth time. All preparations and costs were born by the landowner at the time, and it came to light that this was indeed a condition of the lease by Eastwick Farm that any tenant of the land should keep the gibbet in good repair. It was a grim and misty day and only a handful of spectators arrived to see this historic landmark erected again, although members of the community had spoken out in support of the gibbet and it seems that by this time it was such a constant in the psyche of residents that no one wanted to see the horizon without the gibbet. In 1991 the post was burned down. It's not known who did this or why and was reported as an act of vandalism, but the following year, in 1992, the seventh gibbet post was erected.

Combe Gibbet was immortalised in more ways than one. In 1948 John Schlesinger, who would go on to win Oscars for film directing, produced a black-and-white silent film while at university, called *Black Legend*, shot around the Combe Gibbet and telling the story of this most remarkable murder and punishment.

Our obsession with death and murder never wanes and we love a good grisly artefact. Cabinets of curiosities are becoming popular again. Whitby Museum has the only known surviving 'hand of glory' in Britain. Found in the wall of a thatched cottage in Castleton, Derbyshire, and gifted to the museum in 1937, a hand of glory was a preserved and pickled right hand of a felon, cut off while he hung from the gibbet. The hand was used by burglars in bizarre superstitious rituals. For example, housebreakers would cover the fingers of the hand in human fat and then light the fingers like candles; if one finger refused to light it was a sign that someone in the house was awake. The burglars would also use the hand once inside the house to (theoretically) send inhabitants into a coma so they could carry out their thieving without the possibility of being discovered; such was the power of the hand of glory.

This fascination remains today; we still have the desire to remember macabre things from our collective past, and to preserve them for future generations. The pamphlet detailing the crime and trial of John Keale was gifted to Lincoln library in 1900 by a private collector and still is held at the library today. The original letter from the donator of the booklet is secured in the back of the pamphlet still, and reads:

146

377 James Reckett Avenue, Hull
10th August 1900

Dear sir,
My mother has asked me to write you respecting a booklet giving the history of a man believed to be the last person gibbeted at Lincoln prison. The local museum curator says he thinks you will be interested in some of it so my mother will be pleased to give it into your care. I believe the booklet is about 200 years old. If you are interested will you write me at the above address and I will see the booklet is forwarded.
Yours faithfully
Florence Buxton (Miss)

Gibbeting has even been recorded in song. In 1999 a Lincoln folk group, Da Capo, recorded 'The Tale of Tom Otter'. While I was browsing a second-hand bookshop in Lincoln, researching the many stories of gibbetings for this book, I chatted to the owner about the gibbet and he cheerfully remarked, 'Ah yes, Tom Otter, a friend of mine wrote a song about him for this year's folk festival.' Tom Otter, like so many gibbeted men, has been immortalised and his name still whispers through our casual conversations all these years later. And sometimes the strength of feeling about what may or may not have happened all those years ago is still surprisingly strong.

In 2012 a memorial plaque was unveiled by the mayor of South Tyneside at Jarrow. The last man to have been gibbeted in the north east is now remembered with sympathy, and historians believe he was made a scapegoat for his intention to join the miners' strike. His accomplice, Armstrong, who was cited as dealing the deathly blow to the victim, escaped and is thought to have made a new life for himself abroad. Whatever Jobling did or didn't do, he is not seen as a brutal criminal today and certainly not as deserving the punishment he received. The inscription on the plaque reads:

This was the site of The Gaslight public house, formerly The Commercial, one of the oldest pubs in Jarrow. Legend has it that William Jobling, one of the last men in Britain to be executed and then gibbeted, was brought here after his death in 1832 and secretly buried somewhere by his friends and family.

The last man to be gibbeted in the north east is remembered and given dignity and some grace. But is this fair? At the trial of Jobling witnesses told of how drunk he was and how he had shouted 'kill him' as Armstrong did exactly that. Although the victim, Nichols Fairles, went to great lengths to impress the fact that it was Armstrong and not Jobling who beat him, Jobling was still guilty of being closely involved in murder. Earlier that same evening the pair had accosted John Foster asking for money for drink. Foster gave them some money and the pair moved on. It's hard to say what they would have done if Foster had refused like Fairless did. All these years later, the debate continues. There are those who support Jobling and believe he was a scapegoat, and there are those in the opposite camp who see him as a drunk and a murderer.

The plaque erected to the memory of William Jobling is one of many memorials to these gibbeted men throughout the country. Nicholas Fairles, in contrast, was buried in an unmarked grave at St Hilda's churchyard and no record of the location of the grave was made. There are no memorials to the victims of these crimes. Other than by their own families and sometimes as a detail in the stories of gibbetings, the victims of these terrible crimes are not remembered.

Our libraries hold pamphlets and books detailing the crimes, trials, and punishments of gibbeted men, some of these from the time of the actual murders. Our museums display calling cards, subpoenas, last letters from prison, irons that once held the bodies of rotting criminals, and even the skulls of murderers. We keep their names in streets and landmarks, we even preserve gibbet posts. Gibbeting may be over, but it remains a grisly fascination and something we think of with wonder and a compelling discomfort – and sometimes with guilt.

As the long and dark shadow of the gibbet still stretches over our landscape and our memory, we cannot shake the wonder of this most peculiar form of post-mortem punishment. The irons creak in the wind still, the corpses of executed criminals swing from their bitter old posts. The image of the bird-pecked corpse encased and hanging high on hills and at the turn of busy roads is all too easily conjured up. The horror of the gibbet is gone from our lives, but it remains a most gruesome piece of our history.

Bibliography

Books

Hartshorne, A. (1891) *Hanging In Chains,* Cassell

Walker, R. (1752) *Authentick Memoirs of the Wicked Life and Transactions of Elizabeth Jeffryes, printed and sold by the author*

Baring-Gould, S. (1900) *Yorkshire Oddities, Incidents and Strange Events,* Methuen

Bernard Saunders, W.H. (1888) *Legends and Traditions of Huntingdonshire,* General Books LLC

Andrews, W. (1899) *Bygone Punishments,* Phillip Allan Publishing

Jerdan, W. Ring Workman, W. Morley, J. Arnold, F. Wycliffe Goodwin, C. (1832) *The Literary Gazette: A Weekly Journal of Literature, Science, and the Fine Arts*

Wade, S. (2013) *Yorkshire Murders & Misdemeanours,* Amberley Publishing

Dyndor, Z. (2015) *The Gibbet in the Landscape,* Palgrave Macmillan

Tarlow, S. (2017) *The Golden and Ghoulish Age of the Gibbet in Britain,* Palgrave Macmillan

Online Resources

opengravesopenminds.com
UKmythology.wordpress.com
Parsondrove.net
Farnhamherald.com
wisbechstandard.co.uk
capitalpunishmentuk.org
East Anglian Daily Times

Eastern Daily Express
porttowns.port.ac.uk
drivethedales.com
chevingolf.co.uk
hungerfordvirtualmuseum.co.uk
executedtoday.com
The Newgate Calendar
somersetlive.co.uk
saxilbyhistory.org
invisibleworks.co.uk
legendarydartmoor.co.uk
Leicester Mercury
Stoney Middleton Heritage
paternoster.orpheusweb.co.uk
geriwalton.com
co-curate.ncl.ac.uk
johnknifton.com
ourhertfordandware.org.uk
Watford Observer
georgianera.wordpress.com
lastdyingwords.com
criminalcorpses.com
coflein.gov.uk
spookyisles.com
thewildpeak.wordpress.com
api.parliament.uk